# Timeless Treasures

## The Complete Book On Rotary Cutting

### Nancy Johnson-Srebro

Cover
Migration©
62 1/2" x 62 1/2"
Designed and pieced by Nancy Johnson-Srebro
Quilted by Debbie Grow
The center medallion of Migration© has over
1600 miniature pieces.
The miniature geese are 1/2" x 1".
101 colors were used.

Printed in the United States of America by
Reed Hann Litho Company
Cover photo by Steve Appel, all other photos by Scott Mowry

**RCW**
PUBLISHING COMPANY

Timeless Treasures©
©1992 Nancy Johnson-Srebro
RCW Publishing
Rebecca C. Wilber RR#3, Old Post Lane
Columbia Crossroads, PA 16914-9535  (717) 549-3331

ISBN 0-9627646-3-9
Library of Congress Catalog Card Number: 92-61669

# Acknowledgments

Special thanks to:

Debbie Grow, Laurie Mace and Karen Brown for their countless hours of work in support of this book.

Romayne Bonk and Marcia Bennitt for their special friendship.

James Brogan, who freely gave his time to teach me everything I know about computers.

The quilting group, "Always In Stitches", who encourage me to try out my quilting ideas on them.

Peggy and Randy Schafer, whose dedication to producing quality products has benefited quiltmakers everywhere.

Carol Smith and Jeanne Wilber for the use of their new and antique quilts.

Scott Mowry, for being so accommodating and doing a superb job on the photography.

My husband, Frank, my two sons, Mark and Alan and my daughter, Karen for encouraging me to pursue my quiltmaking career. I couldn't do it without them!

# Dedication

To my maternal Grandmother, Louise Mack Garrison.
Even though you are gone, I think of you daily.
Thank you for instilling the love of quiltmaking in me.

# TABLE OF CONTENTS

# TABLE OF CONTENTS
## -CONTINUED-

# INTRODUCTION

Dear Quilting Friends:

Well, it's been two years since I wrote **Miniature To Masterpiece©**. If anyone had told me then that I would be writing another book, I would not have believed them! I have had the opportunity to travel extensively and talk directly to thousands of quilters. The response to **Miniature To Masterpiece©** has been great. BUT, I still am hearing that there is a need for a book on **complete** rotary cutting, and more patterns with **complete** pressing directions. As many folks know, if you don't press correctly, your quilt or miniature usually doesn't work out.

With this stimulus, I finally took pen in hand and started writing again. In my experience there are only three things that can go wrong with quiltmaking: inaccurate cutting, inaccurate sewing and inaccurate pressing. In this book you will find the answers to overcome these three obstacles.

First, I will give **detailed** information on what type of equipment I use, and a **complete** rotary cutting guide that is geared for **left and right** handed quilters. Second, I will show you with graphics and photos how to get an accurate 1/4"(5mm) seam allowance; and an incredible trick for setting in squares and triangles. Third, I will deal in depth with pressing techniques that will help eliminate problem areas for you. I will share all my secrets!

One of the most important features of this book is the Add On Seam Allowance Chart. You will find this quick reference chart invaluable. I have taken all the guesswork out of determining how much seam allowance to add to eighteen of the most used shapes in quiltmaking. A quick glance at the chart and the answer is right there!

Finally, the most exciting chapter - **The Patterns**! After working with a variety of the 51 patterns in **Timeless Treasures**, you will be an expert at rotary cutting, sewing and pressing. You will be able to make your own Masterpieces!

Thank you for letting me become part of your quilting life. I wish you many hours of contentment, joy and peace while quilting.

Nancy

# THE FORGOTTEN QUILTERS

When I set out to write this book, one of my goals was to make it useful to as many quilters as possible. In my teaching travels I have found that there are two groups that have been sorely neglected when it comes to practical instructions: First - left-handed quilters, and second - the vast majority of people in the world who use the metric system of measurement. So I decided to make a positive impact with both groups.

## LEFT - HANDERS

I have no idea of the percentage of left-handed people in the population, but I must say that it is surely a large number. I've been taking a poll of students in my recent classes, and the number of left-handed people has been running about 15%.

Now, it's easy to say to a left-handed quilter that she/he should just "do the opposite" when it comes to the cutting and piecing instructions. Unfortunately, it isn't so. To get a better perspective on this I taught myself to cut and piece fabric while favoring my left hand. Trying to work "opposite" of the regular instructions just won't do. For example, if the instructions indicate that you should cut on the printed side of the fabric, left-handers do not cut on the wrong side of the fabric. Or should they? This is the dilemma facing our left-handed counterparts.

What really needs to happen is that the left-hander must, at times, work in **mirror image.** Take a look at yourself in the mirror. Your right hand is still on the right, and your left hand is still on the left. But if you are wearing a monogrammed sweater the letters are reversed! This analogy illustrates my point. To be complete, instructions must be written for right-handed quilters and also for left handed quilters. This is what I have done throughout this book. Left-handers will find that the instructions have been written to accommodate you as a primary consideration, not an afterthought.

## THE METRIC WORLD

Although quilting is an American art form, its origin is definitely in the "Old Country". Also, there is very strong interest around the world in quilts in all of their forms, whether quilting is a part of the national heritage or not. Accordingly, it's appropriate to offer patterns in both English and Metric measurements.

Unfortunately, patterns cannot be converted to metric measure by the simple expedient of using a multiplication factor. Seam allowances and others factors enter into the picture and make life complicated for the would-be mathematician. Once again, when I set out to write this book I wanted to make a difference. I had to learn the metric system and begin to think in metric. The result of this work is the instructions and patterns in this volume. The reader will find that all of the patterns are offered in both measurement systems. Those interested in the metric patterns should note that I have rounded all measurements up or down to the nearest 1 millimeter. For instance, 2.34cm will become 2.3cm and 2.35cm will become 2.4cm.

# ROTARY CUTTING EQUIPMENT

After I had operations on my wrists for carpal tunnel syndrome, I had to re-evaluate how I was using my hands and also what type of equipment I was using. I needed equipment that would give me quality cutting but have low stress impact on my hands. Whether you have problems with your hands or not, you will find many helpful ideas in this section. Here is what I have discovered:

### ROTARY CUTTER VERSUS SCISSORS

I am frequently asked by first time students, "Why use a rotary cutter? Why can't I use scissors like my Grandma did?" My reason for using a rotary cutter is ACCURACY. It's not the speed with which you can cut or the fact that you can cut through multi layers; but ACCURACY. I then proceed to show the student what happens when you cut with a rotary cutter versus scissors.

When cutting with a rotary cutter, you don't disturb the fabric. You're not lifting the fabric off the cutting mat. But when you cut with scissors, the fabric is being lifted slightly off the table. You cannot cut a perfect square, etc., even if you have carefully drawn the shape on the fabric. Your hands will not allow you to do this. Every time you cut and stop and then cut again, you will be ever so slightly off. With a rotary cutter, this will not happen. Why? Because you are cutting against a straight edge ruler.

*Fabric lies flat on the mat when cutting with a rotary cutter.*

*When cutting with scissors the fabric does not lie flat on the mat.*

I have tried various name cutters and I keep coming back to the large yellow Olfa™ rotary cutter. This cutter has three features that are best for my hands. *First:* Safety. I like the safety design of this cutter. To open, you gently pull down on the black guard. To close, you simply push the black guard up. If the guard is hard to pull down or push up, **slightly** loosen the screw on the back of the cutter.

By manually opening and closing the cutter yourself, you are the one in control.

*Second:* Size. The size of the Olfa™ cutter fits my hand the best of all the cutters. This is a very important feature to look for when buying a cutter. The bottom of the cutter should fit comfortably in the palm of your hand. If it doesn't, it is either too large or too small for the size of your hand.

*Opening the cutter.*

*Closing the cutter.*

*Cutter in palm of hand*

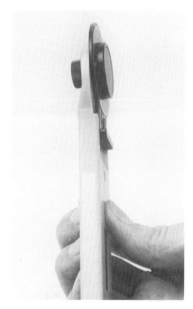

*Etched Ridge on side of cutter*

*Third:* Etched Ridge.
There is an etched ridge on the side of the cutter. This surface was made so your first finger could be placed there.

*Medium green mat reverses to light gray*

Now you have the leverage you need to do cutting. Do not cut with your thumb on the etched ridge, and do not cut with all of your fingers wrapped around the cutter.

Now, practice opening, closing and holding the cutter the proper way. Remember to **always** close the cutter when not using it.

## CUTTING MAT VERSUS VARIOUS CUTTING SURFACES

I shudder every time I see someone walk into class with a piece of plexiglass, wood or linoleum. I just know they are going to tell me this is their cutting mat. If you are cutting on anything other than a nice smooth cutting mat, you are really dulling your $6.00 rotary blade. You are also ruining the piece of plexiglass, wood, etc. Check out the different cutting mats. Since middle age has crept up on me and I had to start wearing glasses for close up work, I find the two color Omnigrid™ mat helps. Light gray on one side, for working with dark fabric, and medium green on the reverse side for when you are working with light fabric.

I also noticed that this mat does not have an odor. Some of the mats I tried had a slight odor to them. Also watch out for mats that appear thicker than an Omnigrid™ mat. I found I could cut deep grooves in these mats. The grooves did not heal properly. After cutting on a mat, you should not be able to see where you have just cut. Also, **always** store your mat in a flat position. Under the bed is a good spot. Don't leave it in direct sunlight or in a cold car overnight. If you do, the mat will buckle and never lie flat again.

## OMNIGRID RULERS VERSUS OTHER RULERS

When Omnigrid™ rulers were introduced on the market, I thought they were the craziest looking things. I was frightened by all the markings, and the yellow lines were beyond my comprehension! I had done extensive work with my existing ruler and was convinced I didn't need any ruler with yellow lines on it.

After buying one and comparing it to my other rulers, I realized all of its advantages.

*First:* These rulers are made for **right or left** handed people! That is why you see **two** sets of numbers on the top and bottom of the ruler. One time I was giving a cutting demonstration to a large group and I forgot to mention this fact. Half way through the demo, I noticed several perplexed looking faces. I proceeded to ask if everyone understood what I had said so far. Finally one woman raised her hand and wanted to know why the numbers on the top and bottom of the ruler read 51, 42, 33, 24 and 15. I could not for the life of me figure out where she was coming up with these numbers. Finally she had to point them out to me. And you know what? She was right! She was reading the numbers up and down **and** I was reading the numbers across!

*Second:* All those markings. For the ultimate in accuracy you really do **need** all those markings. Having the markings in 1/8" (2.5mm) increments, takes the "by guess by golly" out of cutting. You know where you are at all times. I also noticed that the markings don't wear off. I had replaced my previous ruler twice because the markings had worn off over time. So far this hasn't happened on the Omnigrid™ rulers.

*Third:* The yellow lines. The purpose of the yellow lines is to highlight the thin black measuring line. This is invaluable when working on dark Amish solids or dark prints. Some folks tell me they don't know if their fabric should line up with the yellow or black markings. The **black line** is the actual measuring line. Remember the yellow lines are just to highlight the black line. Consequently, you don't want to have your fabric to the left of the yellow line or to the right of the yellow line. If you do, your cutting will be either larger or smaller then the desired size.

*Fourth:* The ruler comes in various sizes. Omnigrid™ has a dozen different rulers for sale. Through trial and error I have found the following to be the best sizes. A 6"x 24" (15 x 60cm) for cutting long strips, a 6" x 12" (15 x 30cm) because it is less awkward to handle for recutting the long strips, a 6" x 6" (15 x 15cm) with a 3" grid in the upper right hand corner. This little gem is my most used ruler for recutting pieces. With the 1/8" grid there is no way you can be inaccurate. Finally, I use a 15" x 15" square. Omnigrid™ makes three different size squares. The best buy for your money is the 15" ruler and you still can cut up to a 15" square.

The preceding information is what I call "Food For Thought." I have shared with you the types of equipment I use to make my miniatures, wallhangings and my full size miniature quilts. You should, by all means, go forth and do some experimenting to find the equipment that best suits you.

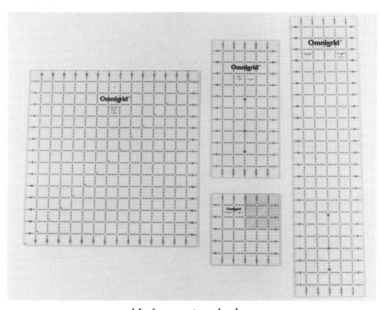

*My four most used rulers*

# STEP ONE

## A Cut Above The Rest - A Rotary Cutting Guide

Now that you have selected the equipment that best meets your cutting needs, it's time to dig in and start cutting! The information in this chapter will answer all the questions I have encountered while working on my own projects, and questions I have been asked by students and fellow quiltmakers.

My friend, Peggy, told me if I was ever going to master rotary cutting, I was going to have to learn to cut both left and right handed. I told her, no way! She said that by the time I was through with a half-yard piece of fabric, I would be able to cut with both hands. She was wrong. It took **one yard** of fabric before I became really good at it! Because of the lessons I learned through this experience I am better able to help left and right handed people perfect their cutting skills. I will show the cutting diagrams for left handed people and then the diagrams for those who are right handed.

For all of the cutting exercises I will cut through two thicknesses of fabric. Rarely will I cut through four layers or more. The reason is simple. The more thicknesses you try to cut through, the more apt the bottom layers are to shift or move on you, causing inaccuracy.

## Cutting A Straight Edge

In this exercise I will use a 6" x 24" (15 x 60cm) Omnigrid™ ruler, a 17" x 23" (43 x 58cm) cutting mat and a one yard piece of fabric, 36" x 44" (91 x 112cm). You may use an equivalent ruler or mat.

To cut a straight edge you first must fold the fabric selvage to selvage. (The selvages are the two tightly woven edges on the material. These edges do not fray. The fabric designer's name is usually printed on the selvage).

The material will now measure 22" x 36" (56 x 91cm). Place it on the cutting mat with the fold at the top (farthest away from you). The selvages will be at the bottom, nearest to you. See Figure 1.

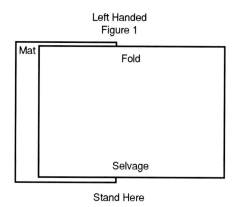

Left Handed
Figure 1

Mat

Fold

Selvage

Stand Here

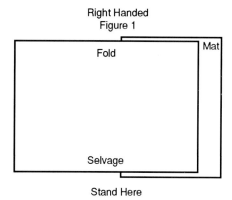

Right Handed
Figure 1

Fold

Mat

Selvage

Stand Here

Now, place the ruler's short side (6" or 15cm) along the fold line. Do this as accurately as you can. The long side (24" or 60cm) will be parallel with the right hand edge for **right** handed people. Similarly, the long side (24" or 60cm) will be parallel with the **left** hand edge for left handed people. See Figure 2.

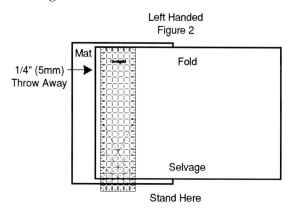

Left Handed
Figure 2

Mat

1/4" (5mm)
Throw Away

Fold

Selvage

Stand Here

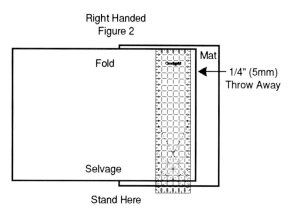

Right Handed
Figure 2

Fold

Mat

1/4" (5mm)
Throw Away

Selvage

Stand Here

Take care to position the ruler edge so that you will only trim a small amount from the edge when you cut. There is no sense in wasting fabric. I usually trim 1/8" (2.5mm) to 1/4" (5mm) off. For the very **first** cut, it **may** not be possible to cut only 1/8" (2.5mm) to 1/4" (5mm). Depending on the washing, drying and how crooked the fabric was cut at the fabric shop, you might have to cut off 1" (2.5cm) or so. Cut off whatever it takes to get a nice straight edge.

If you are **left** handed, place the five finger tips of your right hand on the bottom 6" (15cm) of the ruler. If you are **right** handed, place the five finger tips of your left hand on the bottom 6" (15cm) of the ruler.

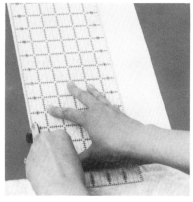

*Left hand cutting*

*Right hand cutting*

Now pick up the rotary cutter and pull the guard back. Place the rotary cutter at the bottom of the fabric (on the selvages, not the fold) with the blade against the ruler. Make sure your first finger is on the etched ridge of the cutter. While keeping pressure on the ruler, start cutting **away from you.  Never towards you.**  I always tell students, it's like driving a car.  You drive much better when you can see what's in front of you. Pulling the rotary cutter towards you is like driving in reverse, which I'm not too good at.

Cut until the rotary cutter is even with your finger tips. Stop cutting.

**Don't** lift the rotary cutter up. While keeping the rotary cutter stationary, carefully move your thumb up to your fingers. Next, press down with your thumb and move your four fingers up the ruler approximately 6" (15cm). Continue cutting until you are again even with your finger tips. Stop cutting. Again keep the rotary blade in the fabric. Carefully move your thumb up to your fingers. Press down. Move your four fingers up the ruler approximately another 6" (15cm). Continue cutting as before. I call this hand walking. By using my hand walking method, you are guaranteed a nice straight cut every time.

### CUTTING A STRAIGHT STRIP

After you have cut a straight edge on the fabric, turn the mat 180°, one half of a full turn. **Do not lift the fabric off the mat.**

If you lift the fabric, instead of turning the mat, you will never be able to get the two straight edges perfectly even again.  You will have defeated yourself in trying to cut a straight edge.  Now, the fold is closest to your body; and the selvage is furthest away from you.  See Figure 3.

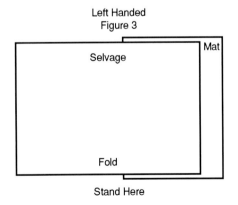

Left Handed
Figure 3

Selvage

Mat

Fold

Stand Here

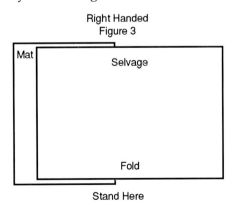

Right Handed
Figure 3

Mat

Selvage

Fold

Stand Here

To continue this exercise, you will begin to cut straight strips. Position the long side of the ruler exactly over the straight edge that you have just cut. Move the ruler until the straight edge of the fabric lines up with the 2 1/2" (6.5cm) marking.  See Figure 4.

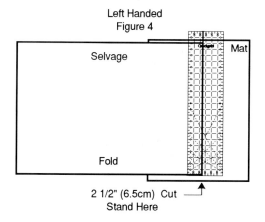

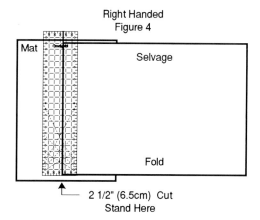

Remember to hold the cutter the proper way and use the hand walking method during the cutting process.  Practice cutting **only** two 2 1/2" (6.5cm) strips.

## RESQUARING THE FABRIC

After cutting two 2 1/2" (6.5cm) strips, I **always** resquare the large piece of fabric.  To do this, just turn the cutting mat 180° (half a turn) and repeat the procedure that you started with.  You should trim the minimum amount, usually no more than 1/8" - 1/4"(2.5mm - 5mm).  See Figures 1-3.  I cannot over-emphasize the importance of this step.  I will never forget the time I was making a Double Irish Chain Quilt.  As this quilt was to be my first **real** quilt, I wanted everything to be perfect.  After squaring up my fabric for the first time, I went "gung ho" into cutting strips.  I cut strips and strips of green fabric.  This didn't seem to be so hard after all!  I was having a grand time.  Needless to say, when I started sewing the strips together, I had a mess.  My green strips had developed what we quilters call a "V" cut at the fold line.

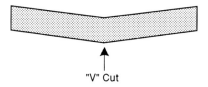

"V" Cut

After countless hours of trying to figure out what went wrong, it dawned on me what had happened.  Your fabric is only "in square" for the width of your ruler.  Referring to Figure 2, we place the 6" (15cm) part of the ruler on the fold.  That means for 6" (15cm) we are "in square."  After 6" (15cm) you must resquare the fabric.  If you do not do this, you will start to accumulate small tolerances that begin to add up.  Within a few cuts, you are no longer cutting at 90° - as compared with the first cut or two.  I personally resquare after every 5" (13cm).

## CUTTING A SQUARE

For the rest of the cutting exercises I will use a 6" x 12" (15 x 30cm) Omnigrid™ ruler. It is half the size of the 6" x 24" (15 x 60cm) ruler and is easier to handle for small cutting jobs. Again, you may use a comparable ruler.

Place one of the 2 1/2" x 22" (6.5 x 56cm) strips on the cutting mat. (Remember the strip is really 2 1/2" x 44" (6.5 x 112cm), but it is folded in half.) Before you can begin cutting squares, you must first square up the edge. You will do this by cutting off the selvages.

For left and right hand cutting, place the short side (6" or 15cm) of the ruler along the top of the strip. See Figure 5. Remember you only want to trim approximately 1/4" (5mm).

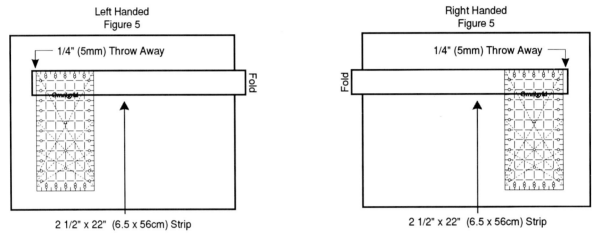

After cutting the selvages, you will turn the cutting mat 180° (half a turn). At this point, most students ask, "How do I get a perfect square?" My answer: Since the strip is 2 1/2" (6.5cm) wide, all you have to do is find the 2 1/2" (6.5cm) marking along the top of the ruler. Place the ruler on top of the fabric so the 2 1/2" (6.5cm) marking lines up perfectly with the newly cut edge. Make sure the top of the ruler is even with the top of the strip. See Figure 6.

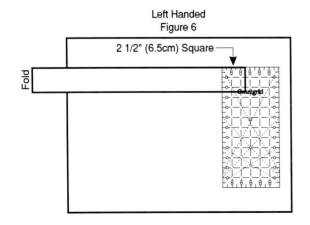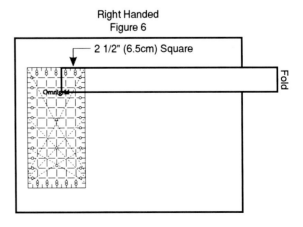

Cut three 2 1/2" (6.5cm) squares. After cutting the three squares, turn the mat 180 degrees (half a turn) and resquare the strip. Turn the mat back 180 degrees so you

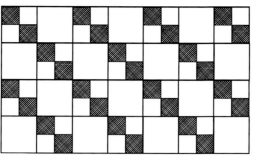

Four Patch Set With Solid Blocks

*You can use squares to make a 4 Patch block, or set them together with solid blocks.*

Four Squares Sewn Together To Make A Four Patch

can continue cutting 2 1/2" (6.5cm) squares. Again, I cannot overemphasize the importance of resquaring the strips. I usually do this after cutting approximately three strips, squares, rectangles, diamonds, etc.

## CUTTING A HALF SQUARE TRIANGLE

After you cut squares, you can easily cut these in half diagonally for half square triangles. This is the method I use for cutting all my triangles. There is no need to use templates. Take the ruler and position it diagonally over the square. See Figure 7. Rotary cut.

Left Handed
Figure 7

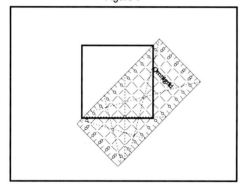

Right Handed
Figure 7

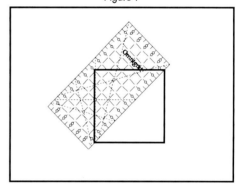

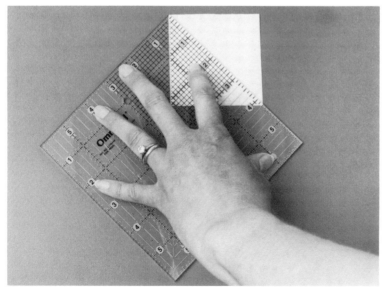

*Cutting a square in half diagonally*

*NOTE: Make sure your first finger tip which is holding the ruler is directly positioned over the fabric triangle that is **underneath** the ruler. I have found if I don't do this, sometimes the fabric triangle moves while I'm cutting it in half diagonally.*

2 Triangles Sewn Together To Make A Square

*A square made from half square triangles is a very versatile block.*

Here are a few of my favorite blocks:

Pinwheel

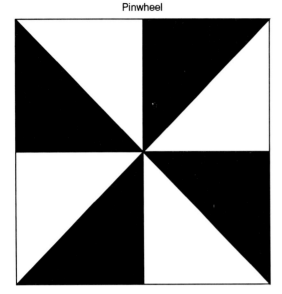

4 Pieced Squares Sewn Together

Jacob's Ladder

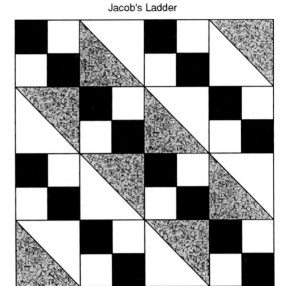

Four Patch Sewn With Pieced Squares

## CUTTING A QUARTER SQUARE TRIANGLE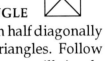

When you cut a 2 1/2" (6.5cm) square in half diagonally **twice**, you will create 4 quarter square triangles. Follow Figure 7 for the first cut. For the second cut, you will simply cut the square in half from the opposite corners. See Figure 7A.

Left Handed
Figure 7A

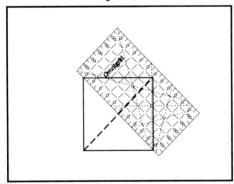

Right Handed
Figure 7A

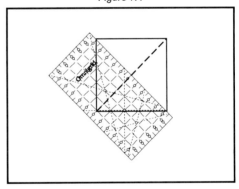

## CUTTING A TRUE RECTANGLE

A true rectangle is a rectangle that is twice as wide as high, or vice versa. For example: a 2" x 4" or 3" x 6" (5 x 10cm or 7.5 x 15cm) rectangle. (An untrue rectangle can be any size. i. e. 4" x 7", 2 1/2" x 10" - 10 x 17.5cm or 6.5 x 25cm) Place one of the 2 1/2" (6.5cm) strips on the mat. Before you can begin cutting rectangles, you must first square up the edge. You will do this by cutting off the selvages. For left and right hand cutting, place the short side of the ruler along the top of the strip. See Figure 8. Only trim approximately 1/4" (5mm).

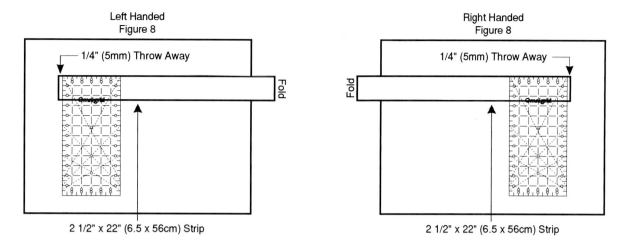

Left Handed
Figure 8

1/4" (5mm) Throw Away

Fold

2 1/2" x 22" (6.5 x 56cm) Strip

Right Handed
Figure 8

1/4" (5mm) Throw Away

Fold

2 1/2" x 22" (6.5 x 56cm) Strip

After cutting off the selvages, turn the mat 180°. You will cut a true rectangle 2 1/2" x 5" (6.5 x 13cm). Remember, you already know the strip is 2 1/2" (6.5cm) wide, so you will find the 5" (13cm) marking on top of the ruler. Place the ruler on top of the fabric so the 5" (13cm) mark lines up perfectly with the newly cut edge. Make sure the top of the ruler is even with the top of the strip. See Figure 9.

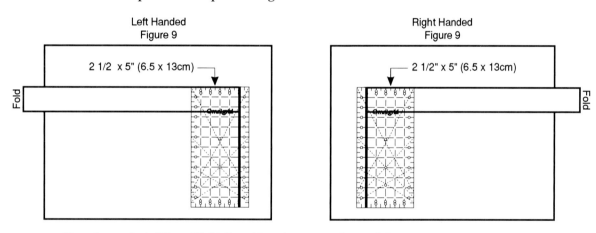

Left Handed
Figure 9

2 1/2 x 5" (6.5 x 13cm)

Fold

Right Handed
Figure 9

2 1/2" x 5" (6.5 x 13cm)

Fold

Cut three 2 1/2" x 5" (6.5 x 13cm) rectangles. After cutting the three rectangles, turn the mat 180° and resquare the strip. Turn the mat back 180° (half a turn) so you can continue cutting rectangles.

Some uses for the rectangle shape are:

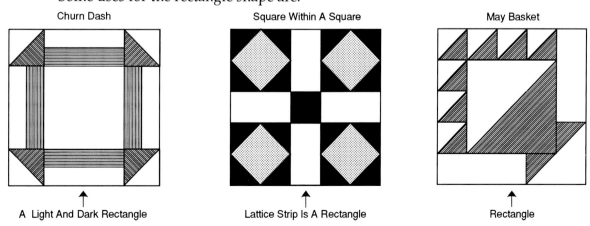

Churn Dash

A  Light And Dark Rectangle

Square Within A Square

Lattice Strip Is A Rectangle

May Basket

Rectangle

## Cutting A True Rectangle In Half

You can just as easily cut true rectangles in half with the same ruler. Take your ruler and position it diagonally over the rectangle. Refer to Figure 10. Rotary cut. To make mirror images of this shape, place two rectangles together, with wrong sides facing each other. Rotary cut.

Left Handed
Figure 10

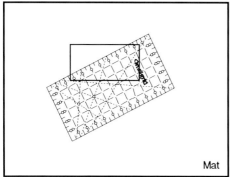

Mat

Stand Here

54 - 40 Or Fight

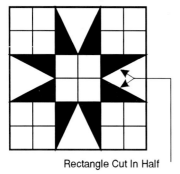

Rectangle Cut In Half

Right Handed
Figure 10

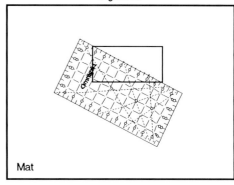

Mat

Stand Here

Storm At Sea Block

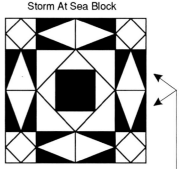

Rectangle Cut In Half

*NOTE: Be sure that the tip of your first finger is pressing on the ruler directly over the fabric that you are cutting. This will keep the fabric from moving while cutting diagonally.*

Some of the most popular blocks using a rectangle cut in half are shown here:

## Cutting Different Angles

Once you master the angles on the Omnigrid™ ruler, the sky is the limit as far as the shapes you can make. I used to cut paper templates and tape them to the underside of the ruler, but I now know this was not necessary. It was not only time consuming, but an error could easily occur while cutting and taping the template to the ruler. Remember: Always try to eliminate templates.

Figure 11

Omnigrid

45°
Mark

Bottom Of The Ruler

## Finding The 45 Degree

Before you begin cutting a 45° diamond, you should study the Omnigrid™ ruler. Figure 11 will show you where the 45° markings are on the ruler.

You will notice there are two 45° lines. One of them slopes from lower left to upper right. The other one slopes from the lower right to the upper left.

Most students are fine up to this point. But when I ask them to turn the ruler to the left 45° marking or the right 45° marking they become confused. A hint I share with students is to place your first finger on the **actual number 45**. Once you do this, it is easy to see the two 45° lines. Practice finding the 45° markings on your ruler. Figure 11A will show you what the ruler will look like turned diagonally. Remember to place your first finger on the number 45.

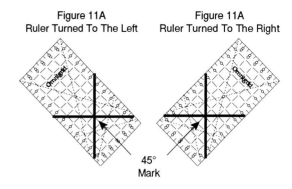

Figure 11A
Ruler Turned To The Left

Figure 11A
Ruler Turned To The Right

45°
Mark

### CUTTING A 45 DEGREE DIAMOND

Place one of the 2 1/2" (6.5cm) strips you previously cut on the mat. Left handed quilters will use the 45° line starting from the lower **left** edge of the ruler. Right handed quilters will use the 45° line starting from the lower **right** edge of the ruler. Place your ruler on the 2 1/2" (6.5cm) strip, making sure the 45° line lines up with the bottom edge of the strip. See Figure 12.

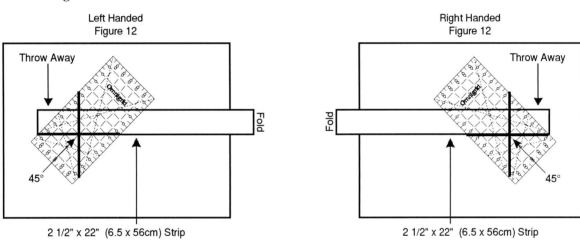

Left Handed
Figure 12

Throw Away

Fold

45°

2 1/2" x 22"  (6.5 x 56cm) Strip

Right Handed
Figure 12

Throw Away

Fold

45°

2 1/2" x 22"  (6.5 x 56cm) Strip

Make the 45° cut. Now turn the mat 180° (half a turn). See Figure 13. This is how your strip should look.

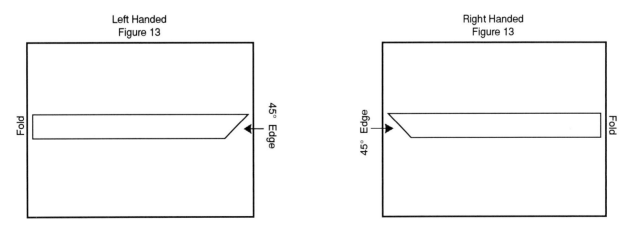

Left Handed
Figure 13

Fold

45° Edge

Right Handed
Figure 13

45° Edge

Fold

Find the 2 1/2" (6.5cm) marking on the top of the ruler. Place the ruler diagonally on the strip so the 2 1/2" (6.5cm) line is on the freshly cut 45° edge. Also make sure the 45° line is on the bottom of the strip. See Figure 14.

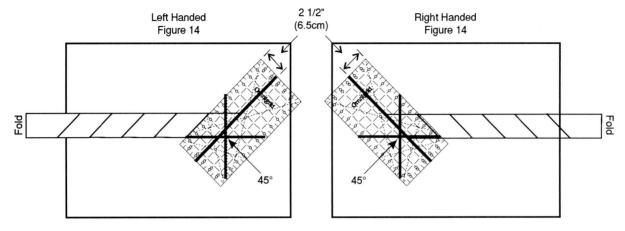

Make the cut and you will have a perfect diamond. To check if you have a true 45° diamond, fold it in half, long point to long point. Everything will match.

After you cut a 45° diamond, use your ruler the same way to make additional 45° cuts. This sure beats drawing around templates and then cutting with scissors!

Many students can handle making a 2 1/2" (6.5cm) diamond, but wonder how to make different size diamonds. This is easy! Remember that your diagonal cuts must be the same as the width of your strip. For example: If you cut a strip of fabric 3 1/4" x 44" (8.25 x 112cm) you will want to make 3 1/4" (8.25cm) diagonal cuts. You will start off as described in Figure 12 and 13, but in Figure 14, you will place the ruler diagonally on the strip so the 3 1/4" (8.25cm) line is on the newly cut 45° edge.

*45° diamonds are widely used throughout quiltmaking. Here are a few examples:*

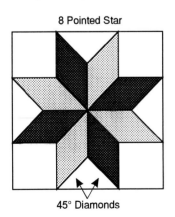

8 Pointed Star

45° Diamonds

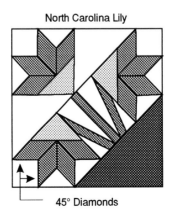

North Carolina Lily

45° Diamonds

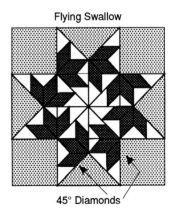

Flying Swallow

45° Diamonds

## CUTTING A PARALLELOGRAM

The hardest part about a parallelogram is the spelling! Actually cutting a parallelogram is much like cutting a 45° diamond.

Place your ruler on a 2 1/2" (6.5cm) strip, making sure the 45° mark lines up with the bottom edge of the strip. See Figure 15.

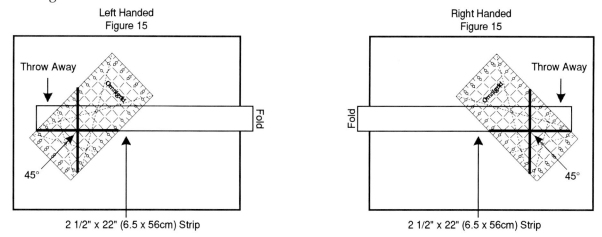

Make the 45° cut. Now turn the mat 180° (half a turn). See Figure 16. This is how your strip should look.

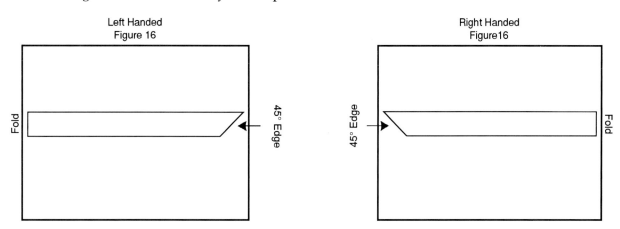

Let's say we want to make a 5" (13cm) diagonal cut. Find the 5" (13cm) marking on the top of the ruler. Place the ruler diagonally on the strip so the 5" (13cm) line is on the freshly cut 45° edge. Also make sure the 45° line is on the bottom of the strip. See Figure 17.

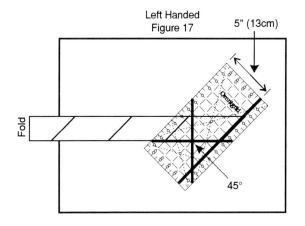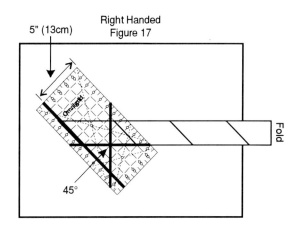

Make the cut and you will have a parallelogram. If you were to fold this piece in half, long point to long point, it will **not** match. So don't get excited! Examples:

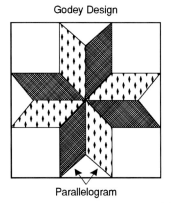

Godey Design

Parallelogram

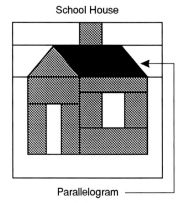

School House

Parallelogram

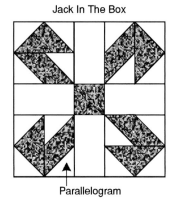

Jack In The Box

Parallelogram

## FINDING THE 60 DEGREE

Again, I want you to study the Omnigrid™ ruler before trying to cut a 60° diamond. Figure 18 will show you where the 60° markings are on the ruler.

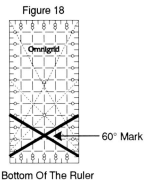

Figure 18

60° Mark

Bottom Of The Ruler

You will notice there are two 60° lines. One of them slopes to the right, and the other to the left. Remember, place your first finger on the **actual number 60.** This way you will be able to see the two 60° lines. Practice finding the 60° markings on the ruler. Figure 18A will show you what the ruler will look like turned diagonally.

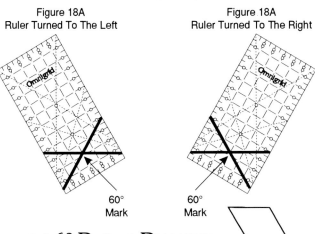

Figure 18A
Ruler Turned To The Left

Figure 18A
Ruler Turned To The Right

60°
Mark

60°
Mark

## CUTTING A 60 DEGREE DIAMOND

Place one of the 2 1/2" (6.5cm) strips on the cutting mat. Left handed quilters will use the 60° line that starts at the lower **left** edge of the ruler. Right handed quilters will use the 60° line that starts at the lower **right** edge of the ruler. Place the ruler on the 2 1/2" (6.5cm) strip, making sure the 60° line lines up with the bottom edge of the strip. See Figure 19.

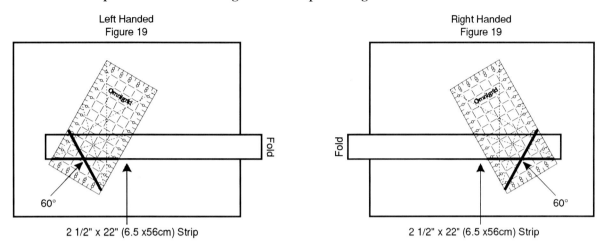

Make the 60° cut. Turn the mat 180° (half a turn). See Figure 20. This is how your strip should look.

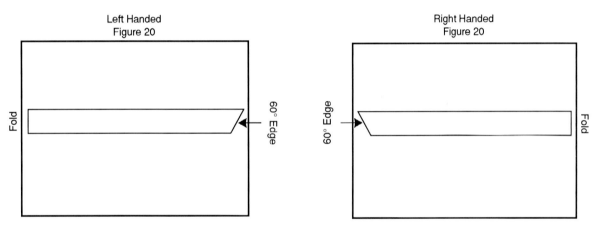

Find the 2 1/2" (6.5cm) marking on the top of the ruler. Place the ruler diagonally on the strip so the 2 1/2" (6.5cm) line is on the newly cut 60° edge. Also make sure the 60° line is on the bottom of the strip. See Figure 21.

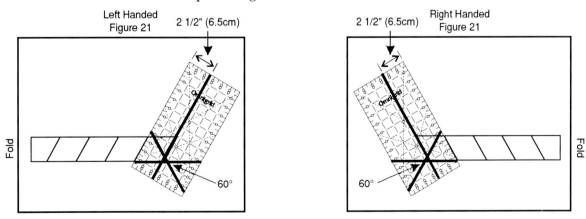

Make the cut and you will have a perfect 60° diamond. To make sure you have a true 60° diamond, fold it in half, long point to long point. Everything will match. Here are examples of two blocks made from 60° diamonds.

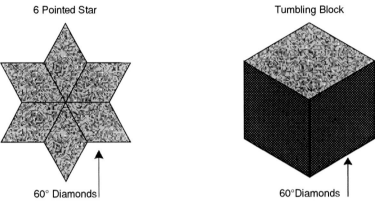

6 Pointed Star                    Tumbling Block

60° Diamonds                      60°Diamonds

After you cut a 60° diamond, line up the ruler the same way to make additional 60° cuts. It is easy to cut different size 60° diamonds.

Whatever size width you cut the strip, that is the size the diagonal cuts have to be. For example: If you cut a strip of fabric 4 1/8" x 44" (10.5 x 112cm) you will want to make 4 1/8" (10.5cm) diagonal cuts. You will start as shown in Figure 19 and 20, but in Figure 21, you will place the ruler diagonally on the strip so the 4 1/8" (10.5cm) line is on the newly cut 60° edge.

## CUTTING A 30 DEGREE DIAMOND

Cutting a 30° diamond is as easy as cutting a 45° diamond. Follow Figures 12, 13, 14 **but use the 30° markings on the ruler.**

## CUTTING A HEXAGON

Cutting a hexagon without templates.....IMPOSSIBLE! Well not anymore. Actually a hexagon is one of the easiest shapes to cut. First, cut a **5" (13cm) 60° diamond.** Yes, that's right, a 60° diamond! Follow Figures 19, 20, 21 but use a 5" (13cm) strip not a 2 1/2" (6.5cm) strip. Now the fun begins.

Place the 60° diamond on the mat so the short points are towards the top and bottom of the mat. The long points will face the sides of the mat. See Figure 22.

For the next step, you must divide the width of the strip in half; 5" divided by 2 equals 2 1/2" (13cm divided by 2 equals 6.5cm). **Left** handed quilters

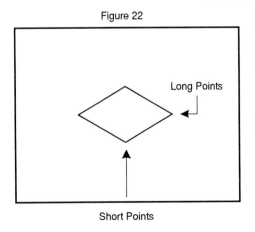

Figure 22

Long Points

Short Points

should position the ruler so the 2 1/2" (6.5cm) line runs through the two **short** points. The 60° line must be on the lower left facet of the diamond. **Right** handed quilters will also position the ruler so the 2 1/2" (6.5cm) line runs through the two **short** points. However the opposite 60° line should be on the lower right facet of the diamond. This may be easily seen in Figure 23. Rotary cut.

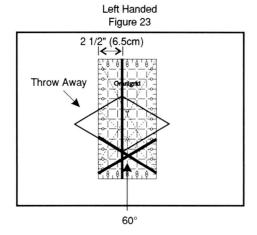

Left Handed
Figure 23

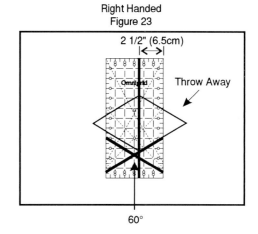

Right Handed
Figure 23

After making the first cut, turn the mat 180° (half a turn) and position the ruler so the 2 1/2" (6.5cm) line again runs through the two **short** points. See Figure 24. Rotary cut. Presto, you have a perfect hexagon!

Left Handed
Figure 24

Right Handed
Figure 24

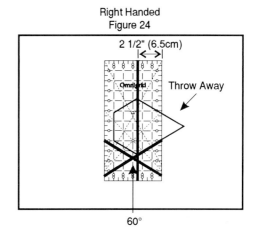

A quick check to insure that you have a perfect hexagon is to measure from one straight edge to another. It will measure 5" (13cm), the original size of the strip. See Figure 25.

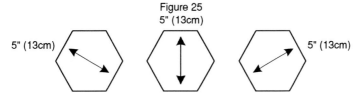

Figure 25
5" (13cm)

You've done it! You have a perfect hexagon. Now you can make as many Grandmother's Flower Garden Quilts as you want. Just remember to divide in half the width of the strip you used to cut the 60° diamond. For example: If the width of the strip was 4" (10cm) and you divided it in half; that would equal 2" (5cm). You would place the 2" (5cm) line through the two short points as shown in Figures 23 and 24. Two blocks using the hexagon shape are shown below.

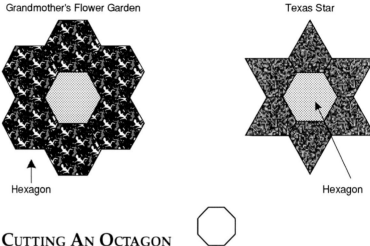

Grandmother's Flower Garden

Texas Star

Hexagon

Hexagon

## CUTTING AN OCTAGON

If I told you an octagon is an eight sided shape and you were going to cut it from a square, would you believe me? I didn't think so! This shape is as easy to cut as the hexagon.

Figure 26

5" (13cm) Square

Start with a 5" (13cm) square. Place it diagonally on the mat so the **wrong** side is facing you. With a pencil lightly draw a diagonal line from point to point across the square twice. See Figure 26.

Once again, you must use one half the width of the strip; 5" (13cm) divided by 2 equals 2 1/2" (6.5cm). For **left** handed quilters, position the ruler so the 2 1/2" (6.5cm) line is on top of the vertical pencil line. **Right** handed quilters should do the same. See Figure 27. Rotary cut.

Left Handed
Figure 27

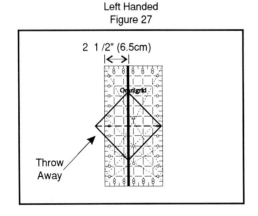

2 1/2" (6.5cm)

Throw
Away

Right Handed
Figure 27

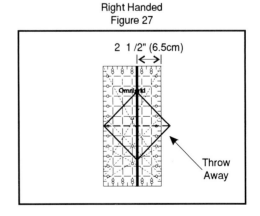

2 1/2" (6.5cm)

Throw
Away

Turn the mat 180° (half a turn) and position the ruler so the 2 1/2" (6.5cm) line again covers the same vertical pencil line. See Figure 28. Rotary cut.

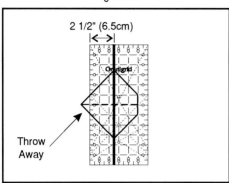

Left Handed
Figure 28

2 1/2" (6.5cm)
|←→|

Throw
Away

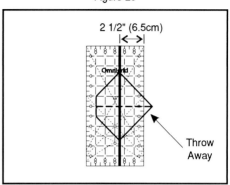

Right Handed
Figure 28

2 1/2" (6.5cm)
|←→|

Throw
Away

You will now have this odd looking shape. See Fig. 29.

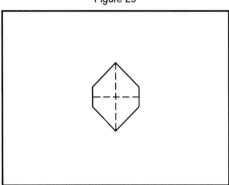

Figure 29

Turn the mat 90° (**a 1/4 turn**). Position the ruler so the 2 1/2" (6.5cm) line runs over the new vertical pencil line. See Figure 30. Rotary cut.

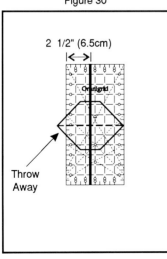

Left Handed
Figure 30

2 1/2" (6.5cm)
|←→|

Throw
Away

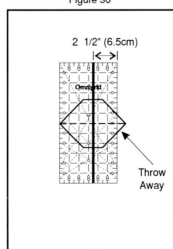

Right Handed
Figure 30

2 1/2" (6.5cm)
|←→|

Throw
Away

Turn the mat 180° (half a turn) and cut off the last point. See Figure 31. You now have a perfect octagon.

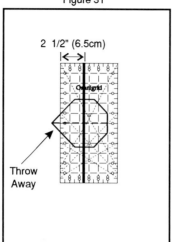

Left Handed
Figure 31

2 1/2" (6.5cm)

Throw Away

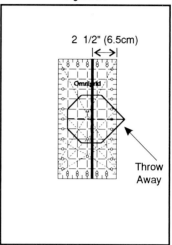

Right Handed
Figure 31

2 1/2" (6.5cm)

Throw Away

If you were to measure from one straight edge to the other, you will find it is 5" (13cm); the original size of the square! See Figure 32.

Figure 32

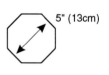

5" (13cm)        5" (13cm)                                        5" (13cm)

5" (13cm)

Examples of the octagon used in different blocks.

Melon Patch

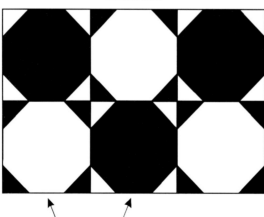

Octagons

Star

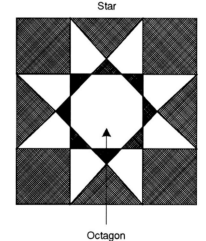

Octagon

## CUTTING AN EQUILATERAL TRIANGLE

When I showed my husband the Thousand Pyramid shapes I had cut with my rotary cutter and ruler, he said, "What great looking equilateral triangles." I had no idea what an equilateral triangle was. I just knew that all three sides had to be the same length in order to piece my Thousand Pyramid miniature. I was really impressed with myself! The more I travel and teach; the more I hear the same thing from the students. They have no idea what an equilateral triangle is. Once I refer to the Thousand Pyramid shape, they instantly know what I'm talking about. Consequently, I try not to use uncommon words when I teach because they are too confusing. It's been years since most students took geometry. My philosophy is: *Keep the definition simple and use as many graphics as you can*. Most students relate to this really well. Again, an equilateral triangle is a triangle with all three sides of equal length. See Figure 33.

Figure 33

Cutting an equilateral triangle is done simply by rotating the ruler. See Figure 34. Left handed quilters will rotate between the two 60° markings on the left side of the ruler. Right handed quilters will rotate between the two 60° markings on the right side of the ruler. Locate these markings on the ruler. Remember to place your first finger on the number 60.

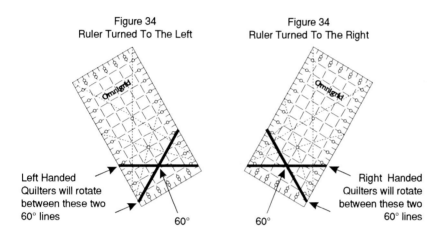

Figure 34
Ruler Turned To The Left

Figure 34
Ruler Turned To The Right

Left Handed Quilters will rotate between these two 60° lines

60°

60°

Right Handed Quilters will rotate between these two 60° lines

Place a 2 1/2" (6.5cm) strip on the mat. Left handed quilters will use the 60° line starting from the lower **left** edge of the ruler. Right handed quilters will use the 60° line starting from the lower **right** edge of the ruler. Place the ruler on the 2 1/2" (6.5cm) strip, making sure the 60° mark lines up with the bottom edge of the strip. See Figure 35. Rotary cut.

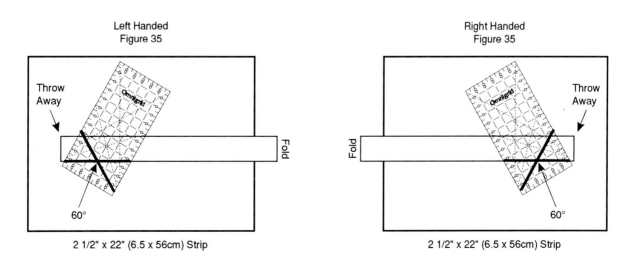

Left Handed
Figure 35

Right Handed
Figure 35

Throw Away

Throw Away

Fold

Fold

60°

60°

2 1/2" x 22" (6.5 x 56cm) Strip

2 1/2" x 22" (6.5 x 56cm) Strip

This is how the strip should look after the cut. **Do not turn the mat.** See Figure 36.

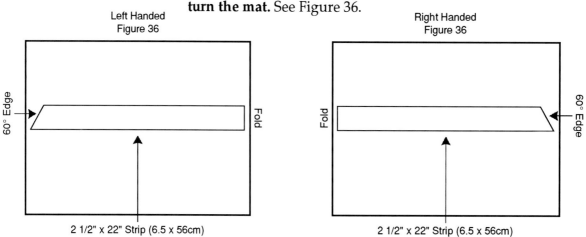

Left Handed
Figure 36

60° Edge

Fold

2 1/2" x 22" Strip (6.5 x 56cm)

Right Handed
Figure 36

Fold

60° Edge

2 1/2" x 22" Strip (6.5 x 56cm)

Keeping your finger on the number 60, rotate the ruler so the other 60° line is now on the bottom of the 2 1/2" (6.5cm) strip. **Left** handed quilters will carefully slide the ruler to the right of the strip, until the ruler lines up with the sharp point of the original cut. Similarly, **right** handed quilters will carefully slide the ruler to the left of the strip until the ruler lines up with the sharp point of the original cut. See Figure 37. Rotary cut.

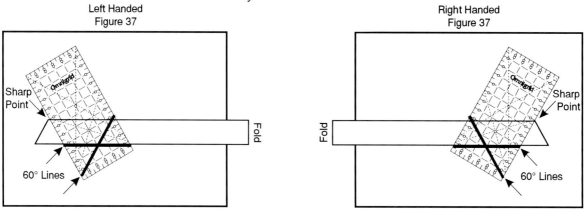

Left Handed
Figure 37

Sharp Point

Omnigrid

60° Lines

Fold

Right Handed
Figure 37

Fold

Omnigrid

Sharp Point

60° Lines

To cut additional equilateral triangles, just rotate the ruler back to the **other** 60° line as in Figure 35. Figure 38 shows several cut equilateral triangles.

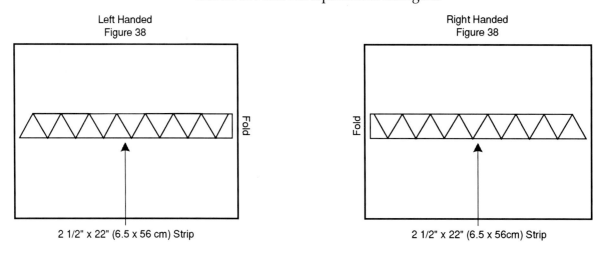

Left Handed
Figure 38

Fold

2 1/2" x 22" (6.5 x 56 cm) Strip

Right Handed
Figure 38

Fold

2 1/2" x 22" (6.5 x 56cm) Strip

Two examples are the Thousand Pyramid Block and a border using 60° equilateral triangles:

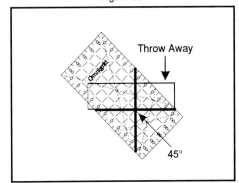

A Border Made of Equilateral Triangles

To cut 45° and 30° triangles (not equilateral), refer to Figures 35-37 but use the appropriate degree lines, i.e. 45° or 30° markings.

Dark and Light
Equilateral Triangles

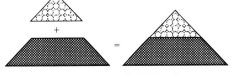

## CUTTING A FULL TRAPEZOID

What an intimidating word. While I was doing research for this chapter, I discovered I had been cutting these shapes called trapezoids for years and didn't know it! In my mind I had classified this shape in two ways: First - a triangle with the upper tip cut off. Second - a rectangle with the sides cut off at an angle. Guess what? That's what they are - full trapezoids! See the examples below:

Two Triangles Sewn To Each Side Of A Trapezoid

Trapezoid Sewn To A Triangle

Cutting this shape is very easy. Cut a 2 1/2" x 9" (6.5 x 22.9cm) rectangle. (Refer to Figures 8 and 9 for cutting a rectangle). Place the rectangle on the mat. **Left** handed quilters will use the 45° marking starting from the lower **left** edge of the ruler. **Right** handed quilters will use the 45° marking starting from the lower **right** edge of the ruler. Place your ruler on the 2 1/2" (6.5cm) strip, making sure the 45° line lines up with the bottom edge of the strip. Notice you are starting your cut at the left **or** right corner. See Figure 39. Rotary cut.

Left Handed
Figure 39

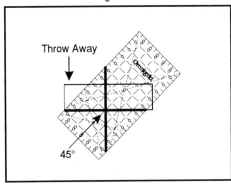

Throw Away

45°

Right Handed
Figure 39

Throw Away

45°

Now turn the mat 180° (half a turn). See Figure 40. This is how your strip should look.

Left Handed
Figure 40

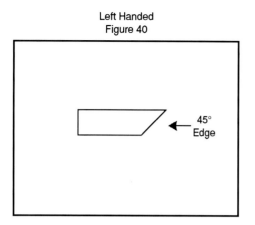

45°
Edge

Right Handed
Figure 40

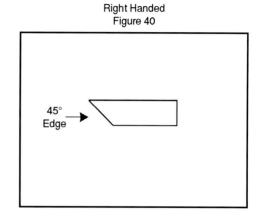

45°
Edge

Place the ruler so the 45° line runs along the bottom of the strip.

Also make sure the ruler edge is lined up diagonally with the **top** corner of the rectangle. See Figure 41. Rotary cut.

Left Handed
Figure 41

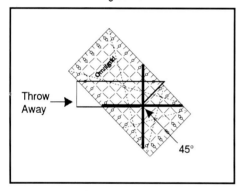

Throw Away

45°

Right Handed
Figure 41

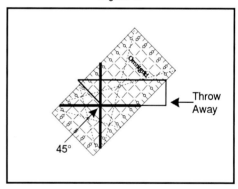

Throw Away

45°

Now you have a perfect full trapezoid. See Figure 42.

Figure 42

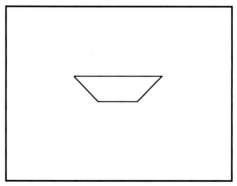

A Full Trapezoid

To ensure you have a true trapezoid, fold it in half, point to point. Everything will match. Some examples of quilt blocks that use a full trapezoid:

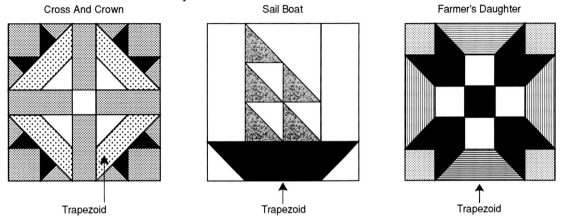

Cross And Crown        Sail Boat        Farmer's Daughter

Trapezoid        Trapezoid        Trapezoid

## CUTTING A RIGHT HALF OR LEFT HALF TRAPEZOID

To make a half trapezoid, you will only make **one diagonal cut**. Your quilt pattern will determine if it is a right or left half trapezoid. Refer to Figure 39 **OR** Figure 41 to make the appropriate cut.

Figure 43 will show you what a right half trapezoid and a left half trapezoid looks like.

Figure 43

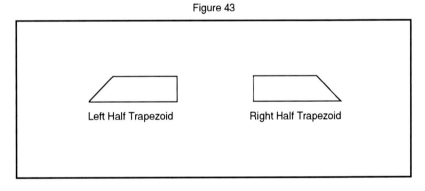

Left Half Trapezoid        Right Half Trapezoid

I think the most popular use for this shape is the Attic Window pattern. Examples of the Attic Window Block:

Four Attic Window Blocks

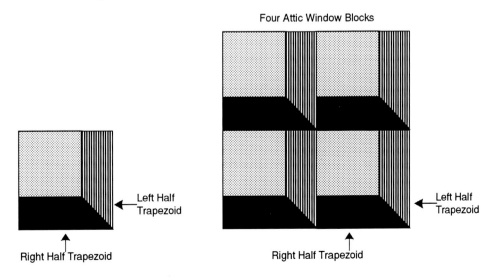

Left Half Trapezoid

Left Half Trapezoid

Right Half Trapezoid        Right Half Trapezoid

Star And Cross

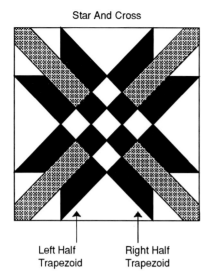

Left Half
Trapezoid

Right Half
Trapezoid

King's Crown

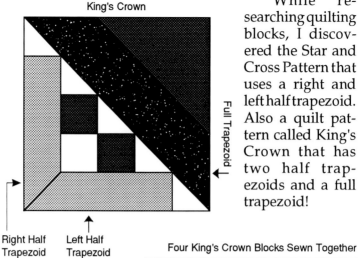

Full Trapezoid

Right Half
Trapezoid

Left Half
Trapezoid

While researching quilting blocks, I discovered the Star and Cross Pattern that uses a right and left half trapezoid. Also a quilt pattern called King's Crown that has two half trapezoids and a full trapezoid!

I didn't think the King's Crown block was very impressive looking until I sewed four blocks together. The result is very dramatic, and you can cut everything without templates.

Four King's Crown Blocks Sewn Together

## CUTTING ODD SHAPES

### THE KITE SHAPE

Every once in a while in quiltmaking, I come across a pattern that requires an odd shaped piece. One such shape is known as a kite.

I encountered this shape when designing a Feathered Star quilt. After some trial and error, I discovered it was quite easy to cut. First, cut a 5" (13cm) square. (Refer to Figure 5 and 6 for cutting a square). Second, cut the square in half diagonally. (Refer to Figure 7). Now you will have a triangle. Position the triangle on the mat so the longest side is away from your body. See Figure 44.

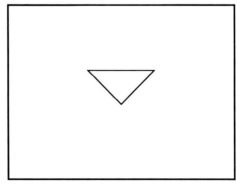

Figure 44

Next, find the 5" (13cm) marking on the ruler. (You will use the 5" (13cm) marking because that was the size of the original square.) Place the top of the ruler so it aligns with the top of the triangle, and the tip of the triangle is on the 5" (13cm) line. See Figure 45. Rotary cut.

Left Handed
Figure 45

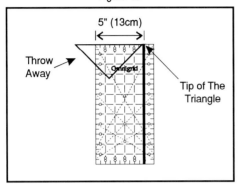

Right Handed
Figure 45

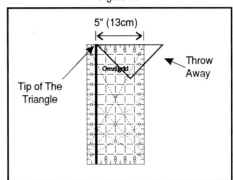

Now you have a perfectly cut kite shape. See Figure 46.

Left Handed
Figure 46

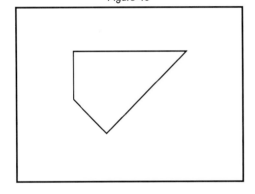

Right Handed
Figure 45

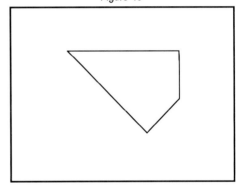

I use this kite shaped piece for my Feathered Star pattern. Three different looking Feathered Star blocks are shown below:

Kite Shape

Kite Shape

Kite Shape

I wondered what would happen if I sewed eight of these kite shapes together. See Figure 47.

Figure 47

To my surprise, I came up with a pieced octagon! This pieced octagon proved to be very versatile since you may create many different blocks with it.

The following are just three different color combinations I designed while piecing four blocks together.

Figure 48

### THE DOUBLE PRISM SHAPE

My first encounter with this shape (see Figure 48) was several years ago when I decided to sew my Mariner's Compass blocks with a Garden Maze setting. (I must confess, I made a cardboard template of this shape and drew around it!) A few years later when I was working on a miniature, I remembered the Garden Maze setting. Only this time I was determined to find a way to eliminate the cardboard template.

Figure 49

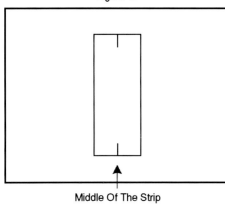

Middle Of The Strip

To cut this shape, you will cut a 5" x 12" (13 x 30cm) rectangle. (Refer to Figures 8 and 9 for cutting a rectangle). Next, divide the width of the rectangle in half: 5" divided by 2 is 2 1/2" (13 divided by 2 is 6.5cm). With the ruler, measure in from the side of the rectangle 2 1/2" (6.5cm) and place a small pencil mark on the top and bottom of the rectangle. See Figure 49.

Place the ruler so the 45° marking runs through the 2 1/2" (6.5cm) pencil mark. See Figure 50. Rotary cut.

Left Handed
Figure 50

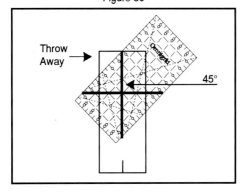

Throw Away

45°

Right Handed
Figure 50

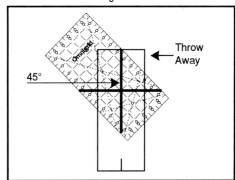

Throw Away

45°

Turn the mat 90° **(1/4 turn)** and place the ruler so the opposite 45° marking runs through the 2 1/2" (6.5cm) pencil mark. See Figure 51. Rotary cut.

Left Handed
Figure 51

Right Handed
Figure 51

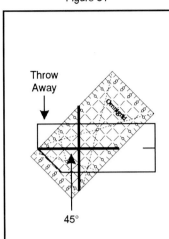

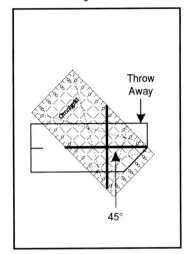

You have now successfully cut the top half of a Double Prism Shape. To finish cutting the bottom half, repeat the steps shown in Figures 50 and 51.

## THE PRISM SHAPE

To make the Prism shape, you will cut **only one end** of the rectangle. Follow Figures 49, 50 and 51. Three examples of this shape used in quiltmaking:

Nonesuch

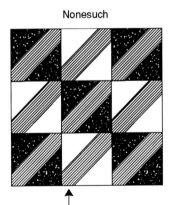

Double Prism

Garden Maze

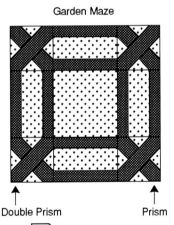

Double Prism          Prism

Bachelor's Puzzle

Prism

## CUTTING A CLIPPED SQUARE

While working on patterns for this book, I came across a shape I named clipped square. It is so named because you "clip off " the corner of a square.

You must first draw the pattern on graph paper to determine how much of the square you want clipped off. Then add 1/4" (5mm) to the diagonal clip for the seam allowance. Now draw a diagonal line from corner to corner on the square. See Figure 52.

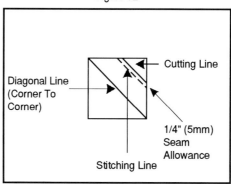
Figure 52

To determine the **correct** amount to cut off, measure from the diagonal line to the cutting line. To cut the excess off, simply turn the square on the mat and position the ruler so the **correct** measurement runs through the diagonal line. For the example I will use 1 1/2" (3.8cm) for the **correct** measurement. Cut off the excess corner. See Figure 53.

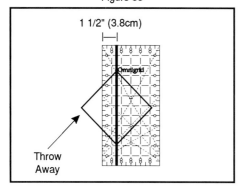

Left Handed
Figure 53

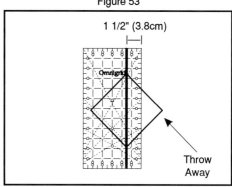

Right Handed
Figure 53

I used this method for the Bow Tie and Blazing Star blocks.

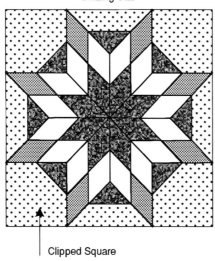
Blazing Star

Clipped Square

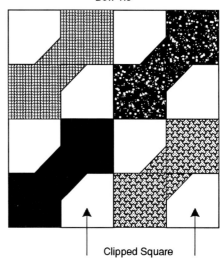
Bow Tie

Clipped Square

## SQUARING UP A BLOCK

No matter how careful you are in cutting, sewing and pressing, there are times when the quilt block is **slightly** out of square. To square up a miniature block, I use the 6" x 6" (with 3" grid) ruler. For larger blocks I use the 15" x 15" ruler.

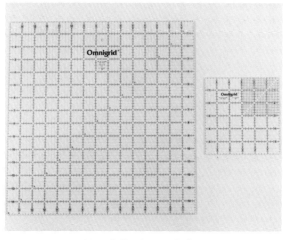

*6" and 15" Square Rulers*

First turn the ruler upside down.

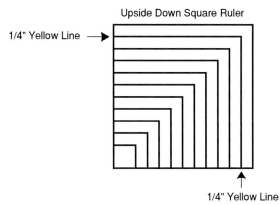

Upside Down Square Ruler

1/4" Yellow Line →

← 1/4" Yellow Line

You will see a yellow line that runs on the bottom, turns the corner, and runs down the left side of the ruler. This is the 1/4" line. (The ruler has solid yellow lines spaced every quarter inch).

I will use an eight pointed star block for demonstration. Place the ruler on top of the star block so the star points on the top and right side of the block are touching this 1/4" yellow line.

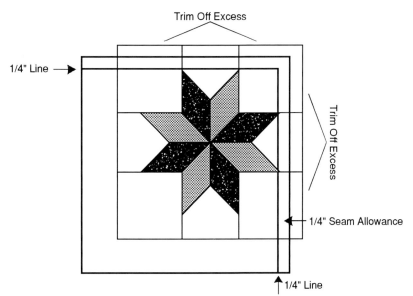

Trim Off Excess

1/4" Line →

Trim Off Excess

1/4" Seam Allowance

1/4" Line

Trim any extra material hanging over the top and right side of the ruler. Be **very careful** when trimming. **Always** make sure you have a 1/4" seam allowance. Turn the block 180° and trim the remaining two sides.

# ENGLISH AND METRIC
# "ADD ON SEAM ALLOWANCE" CHART

*Now that you are familiar with how to rotary cut different shapes, it is important to be able to determine the proper seam allowance to add to each of these shapes. A priority when I started this book was to develop this simple, but easy to use, "Add On Seam Allowance" chart.*

Here's how to use the chart:

1. Simply substitute your desired FINISHED size where my size is stated.
2. Referring to the chart, add the appropriate seam allowance measurement to your FINISHED size.
3. You now know the correct size to rotary cut this shape. This is also the correct size if you want to cut templates for your pattern pieces.

## ENGLISH
### ADD ON SEAM ALLOWANCE CHART
(Based upon using 1/4" seam allowance)

**TO CUT A SQUARE**

Add 1/2" to the height and 1/2" to the length of the desired FINISHED size.

EXAMPLE:
Desired FINISHED size: 2" square

Add on seam allowance to the height: 1/2"
    (1/2" + 2" = 2 1/2")
Add on seam allowance to the length: 1/2"
    (1/2" + 2" = 2 1/2")

Size of Square To Cut: 2 1/2" x 2 1/2"
    *See page 16 for cutting how to.*

**TO CUT A HALF SQUARE TRIANGLE**

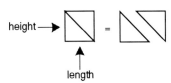

A half square triangle is made from a square cut in half diagonally.

Add 7/8" to the height and 7/8" to the length of the desired FINISHED size of a square made from sewing two half square triangles together. Cut square in half diagonally to obtain a half square triangle.

EXAMPLE:
Desired FINISHED size of a square sewn from two half square triangles: 2"

## METRIC
### ADD ON SEAM ALLOWANCE CHART
(Based upon using 5mm seam allowance)

**TO CUT A SQUARE**

Add 1cm to the height and 1cm to the length of the desired FINISHED size.

EXAMPLE:
Desired FINISHED size: 5cm square

Add on seam allowance to the height: 1cm
    (1cm + 5cm = 6cm)
Add on seam allowance to the length: 1cm
    (1cm + 5cm = 6cm)

Size of Square To Cut: 6cm x 6cm
    *See page 16 for cutting how to.*

**TO CUT A HALF SQUARE TRIANGLE**

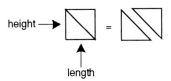

A half square triangle is made from a square cut in half diagonally.

Add 1.75cm to the height and 1.75cm to the length of the desired FINISHED size of a square made from sewing two half square triangles together. Cut square in half diagonally to obtain a half square triangle.

EXAMPLE:
Desired FINISHED size of a square sewn from two half square triangles: 5cm

ENGLISH - To Cut A Half Square Triangle
continued ...

Add on seam allowance to the height: 7/8"
(7/8" + 2" = 2 7/8")
Add on seam allowance to the length: 7/8"
(7/8" + 2" = 2 7/8")

Size of Square To Cut: 2 7/8"
Recut square in half diagonally.
*See page 17 for cutting how to.*

## TO CUT A QUARTER SQUARE TRIANGLE

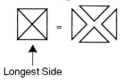

Longest Side

A quarter square triangle is made from a square cut in half diagonally, twice.

Add 1 1/4" to the desired FINISHED size of the longest side of the quarter square triangle.

EXAMPLE:
Desired FINISHED size of the longest side: 3"

Add on seam allowance to the longest side: 1 1/4"
(1 1/4"x 3" = 4 1/4")

Size of Square To Cut: 4 1/4" x 4 1/4"
Recut the square in half diagonally twice.
*See page 18 for cutting how to.*

## TO CUT A TRUE RECTANGLE

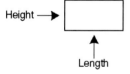

Height →

Length

A true rectangle is always twice as long in length as the height. For example: 2" x 4", 3" x 6", etc.

Add 1/2" to the height and 1/2" to the length of the desired FINISHED size.

EXAMPLE:
Desired FINISHED size: 2" x 4" rectangle

Add on seam allowance to the height: 1/2"
(1/2" + 2" = 2 1/2")
Add on seam allowance to the length: 1/2"
(1/2" + 4" = 4 1/2")

Size of Rectangle To Cut: 2 1/2" x 4 1/2"
*See page 18 for cutting how to.*

METRIC - To Cut A Half Square Triangle
continued ...

Add on seam allowance to the height: 1.75cm
(1.75cm + 5cm = 6.75cm)
Add on seam allowance to the length: 1.75cm
(1.75cm + 5cm = 6.75cm)

Size of Square To Cut: 6.75cm
Recut square in half diagonally.
*See page 17 for cutting how to.*

## TO CUT A QUARTER SQUARE TRIANGLE

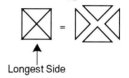

Longest Side

A quarter square triangle is made from a square cut in half diagonally, twice.

Add 2.5cm to the desired FINISHED size of the longest side of the quarter square triangle.

EXAMPLE:
Desired FINISHED size of the longest side: 7.6cm

Add on seam allowance to the longest side: 2.5cm
(2.5cm x 7.6cm = 10.1cm)

Size of Square To Cut: 10.1cm x 10.1cm
Recut the square in half diagonally twice.
*See page 18 for cutting how to.*

## TO CUT A TRUE RECTANGLE

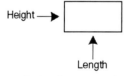

Height →

Length

A true rectangle is always twice as long in length as the height. For example: 5 x 10cm, 10 x 20cm, etc.

Add 1cm to the height and 1cm to the length of the desired FINISHED size.

EXAMPLE:
Desired FINISHED size: 5cm x 10cm rectangle

Add on seam allowance to the height: 1cm
(1cm + 5cm = 6cm)
Add on seam allowance to the length: 1cm
(1cm + 10cm = 11cm)

Size of Rectangle To Cut: 6 x 11cm
*See page 18 for cutting how to.*

**TO CUT A HALF RECTANGLE FROM
A TRUE RECTANGLE**

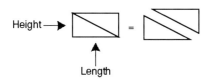

Add 11/16" (11/16" is located between 5/8" and 3/4") to the height of the FINISHED size and 1 1/8" to the length of the FINISHED size.

EXAMPLE:
Desired FINISHED size of a rectangle made from sewing two true half rectangles together: 2" x 4"

Add on seam allowance for height: 11/16"
      (11/16" + 2" = 2 11/16")
Add on seam allowance for length: 1 1/8"
      (1 1/8" + 4" = 5 1/8")

Size of Rectangle To Cut: 2 11/16" x 5 1/8"
Recut in half diagonally.
*See page 20 for cutting how to.*

**NOTE:** This add on seam allowance only works for a
      **true** rectangle.

**TO CUT AN EQUILATERAL TRIANGLE**

Add 3/4" to the height of the desired FINISHED height.

EXAMPLE:
Desired FINISHED height:
      2" high equilateral triangle

Add on seam allowance: 3/4"
      (3/4" + 2" = 2 3/4")

Height of strip to cut: 2 3/4" Use the 60° markings on the ruler to finish cutting the sides.
*See page 30 for cutting how to.*

**TO CUT A HALF RECTANGLE FROM
A TRUE RECTANGLE**

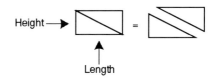

Add 1.4cm to the height of the FINISHED size and 2.3cm to the length of the FINISHED size.

EXAMPLE:
Desired FINISHED size of a rectangle made from sewing two true half rectangles together: 5cm x 10cm

Add on seam allowance for height: 1.4cm
      (1.4cm + 5cm = 6.4cm)
Add on seam allowance for length: 2.3cm
      (2.3cm + 10cm = 12.3cm)

Size of Rectangle To Cut: 6.4 x 12.3cm
Recut in half diagonally.
*See page 20 for cutting how to.*

**NOTE:** This add on seam allowance only works for a
      **true** rectangle.

**TO CUT AN EQUILATERAL TRIANGLE**

Add 1.5cm to the height of the desired FINISHED height.

EXAMPLE:
Desired FINISHED height:
      5cm high equilateral triangle

Add on seam allowance: 1.5cm
      (1.5cm + 5cm = 6.5cm)

Height of strip to cut: 6.5cm. Use the 60° markings on the ruler to finish cutting the sides.
*See page 30 for cutting how to.*

**TO CUT A 30° DIAMOND**

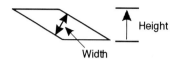

Add 1/2" to the height and 1/2" to the width of the desired FINISHED size.

EXAMPLE:
Desired FINISHED size: a 2"- 30° diamond

Add on seam allowance to the height: 1/2"
    (1/2" + 2" = 2 1/2")
Add on seam allowance to the width: 1/2"
    (1/2" + 2" = 2 1/2")

Height of strip of fabric to cut: 2 1/2"

Using the 30° marking on ruler, recut into 2 1/2" diamonds.
    *See page 26 for cutting how to.*


**TO CUT A 30° DIAMOND**

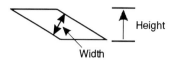

Add 1cm to the height and 1cm to the width of the desired FINISHED size.

EXAMPLE:
Desired FINISHED size: a 5cm - 30° diamond

Add on seam allowance to the height: 1cm
    (1cm + 5cm = 6cm)
Add on seam allowance to the width: 1cm
    (1cm + 5cm = 6cm)

Height of strip of fabric to cut: 6cm

Using the 30° marking on ruler, recut into 6cm diamonds.
    *See page 26 for cutting how to.*


**TO CUT A 45° DIAMOND**

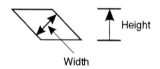

Add 1/2" to the height and 1/2" to the width of the desired FINISHED size.

EXAMPLE:
Desired FINISHED size: a 3"- 45° diamond

Add on seam allowance to height: 1/2"
    (1/2" + 3" = 3 1/2")
Add on seam allowance to width: 1/2"
    (1/2" + 3" = 3 1/2")

Height of strip of fabric to cut: 3 1/2"

Using the 45° marking on ruler, recut into 3 1/2" diamonds.
    *See page 21 for cutting how to.*


**TO CUT A 45° DIAMOND**

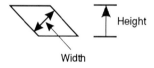

Add 1cm to the height and 1cm to the width of the desired FINISHED size.

EXAMPLE:
Desired FINISHED size: a 6cm - 45° diamond

Add on seam allowance to the height: 1cm
    (1cm + 6cm = 7cm)
Add on seam allowance to the width: 1cm
    (1cm + 6cm = 7cm)

Height of strip of fabric to cut: 7cm

Using the 45° marking on ruler, recut into 7cm diamonds.
    *See page 21 for cutting how to.*

## TO CUT A PARALLELOGRAM

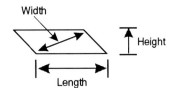

Add 1/2" to the height and 3/4" to the length of the desired FINISHED size.

EXAMPLE:
Desired FINISHED size:
       a 2" (height) x 4"(length) parallelogram

Add on seam allowance for height: 1/2"
       (1/2" + 2" = 2 1/2")
Add on seam allowance for length: 3/4"
       (3/4" + 4" = 4 3/4")

Height of strip of fabric to cut: 2 1/2"

To Find The Width of The Diagonal Cuts: Make a 45° cut. Measure over 4 3/4" from the 45° cut and place a pencil mark at the top of the strip. Turn the ruler diagonally so it lines up both with the 45° cut and the pencil mark. In this case, the width of the diagonal cuts will be 3 3/8".
*See page 22 for cutting how to.*

## TO CUT A PARALLELOGRAM

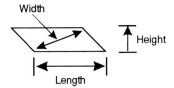

Add 1cm to the height and 1.5cm to the length of the desired FINISHED size.

EXAMPLE:
Desired FINISHED size:
       a 5cm (height) x 10cm (length) parallelogram

Add on seam allowance for height: 1cm
       (1cm + 5cm = 6cm)
Add on seam allowance for length: 1.5cm
       (1.5cm + 10cm = 11.5cm)

Height of strip of fabric to cut: 6cm

To Find The Width of The Diagonal Cuts: Make a 45° cut. Measure over 11.5cm from the 45° cut and place a pencil mark at the top of the strip. Turn the ruler diagonally so it lines up both with the 45° cut and the pencil mark. In this case, the width of the diagonal cuts will be 8cm.
*See page 22 for cutting how to.*

## TO CUT A 60° DIAMOND

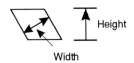

Add 1/2" to the height and 1/2" to the width of the desired FINISHED size.

EXAMPLE:
Desired FINISHED size: a 4"- 60° diamond

Add on seam allowance for height: 1/2"
       (1/2" + 4" = 4 1/2")
Add on seam allowance for width: 1/2"
       (1/2" + 4" = 4 1/2")

Height of strip of fabric to cut: 4 1/2"

Using the 60° marking on ruler, recut into 4 1/2" diamonds.
*See page 24 for cutting how to.*

## TO CUT A 60° DIAMOND

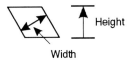

Add 1cm to the height and 1cm to the width of the desired FINISHED size.

EXAMPLE:
Desired FINISHED size: a 7cm - 60° diamond

Add on seam allowance for height: 1cm
       (1cm + 7cm = 8cm)
Add on seam allowance for width: 1cm
       (1cm + 7cm = 8cm)

Height of strip of fabric to cut: 8cm

Using the 60° marking on ruler, recut into 8cm diamonds.
*See page 24 for cutting how to.*

**TO CUT A HEXAGON (A 6 sided shape)**

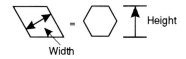

A hexagon is cut from a 60° diamond.

Add 1/2" to the height and 1/2" to the width of the desired FINISHED size.

EXAMPLE:
Desired FINISHED size: 2" hexagon

Add on seam allowance for height: 1/2"
        (1/2" + 2" = 2 1/2")
Add on seam allowance for width: 1/2"
        (1/2" + 2" = 2 1/2")

Height of strip of fabric to cut: 2 1/2"

Using the 60° marking on the ruler, cut into a 2 1/2" diamond. Recut the diamond into a hexagon.
*See page 26 for cutting a hexagon.*


**TO CUT A HEXAGON (A 6 sided shape)**

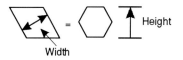

A hexagon is cut from a 60° diamond.

Add 1cm to the height and 1cm to the width of the desired FINISHED size.

EXAMPLE:
Desired FINISHED size: 5cm hexagon

Add on seam allowance for height: 1cm
        (1cm + 5cm = 6cm)
Add on seam allowance for width: 1cm
        (1cm + 5cm = 6cm)

Height of strip of fabric to cut: 6cm

Using the 60° marking on the ruler, cut into a 6cm diamond. Recut the diamond into a hexagon.
*See page 26 for cutting a hexagon.*


**TO CUT AN OCTAGON (An 8 sided shape)**

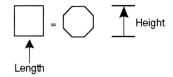

An octagon is cut from a square.

Add 1/2" to the height and 1/2" to the length of the desired FINISHED size.

EXAMPLE:
Desired FINISHED size: 2" octagon

Add on seam allowance to height: 1/2"
        (1/2" + 2" = 2 1/2")
Add on seam allowance to length: 1/2"
        (1/2" + 2" = 2 1/2")

Size of Square To Cut: 2 1/2"
Recut the square into an octagon.
*See page 28 for cutting an octagon.*


**TO CUT AN OCTAGON (An 8 sided shape)**

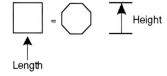

An octagon is cut from a square.

Add 1cm to the height and 1cm to the length of the desired FINISHED size.

EXAMPLE:
Desired FINISHED size: 5cm octagon

Add on seam allowance to height: 1cm
        (1cm + 5cm = 6cm)
Add on seam allowance to length: 1cm
        (1cm + 5cm = 6cm)

Size of Square To Cut: 6cm.
Recut the square into an octagon.
*See page 28 for cutting an octagon.*

## TO CUT A FULL TRAPEZOID

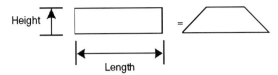

A trapezoid is cut from a rectangle.

Add 1/2" to the height and 1 1/4" to the length of the desired FINISHED size.

EXAMPLE:
Desired FINISHED size: 1 1/2" (height) x 4" (length)

Add on seam allowance for height: 1/2"
    (1/2" + 1 1/2" = 2")
Add on seam allowance for length: 1 1/4"
    (1 1/4" + 4" = 5 1/4")

Size of Rectangle To Cut: 2" x 5 1/4"

Using the 45° marking on ruler, recut into a full trapezoid.
*See page 33 for cutting a full trapezoid.*

## TO CUT A LEFT OR RIGHT HALF TRAPEZOID

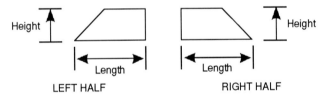

A left or right half trapezoid is cut from a rectangle.

Add 1/2" to the height and 7/8" to the length of the desired FINISHED size.

EXAMPLE:
Desired FINISHED size:
        2"(height) x 5" (length)

Add on seam allowance for height: 1/2"
    (1/2" + 2" = 2 1/2")
Add on seam allowance for length: 7/8"
    (7/8" + 5" = 5 7/8")

Size of Rectangle To Cut: 2 1/2" x 5 7/8"
Using the 45° marking on the ruler, recut into a left or right half trapezoid.
*See page 35 for cutting a half trapezoid.*

## TO CUT A FULL TRAPEZOID

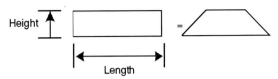

A trapezoid is cut from a rectangle.

Add 1cm to the height and 2.5cm to the length of the desired FINISHED size.

EXAMPLE:
Desired FINISHED size: 4cm (height) x 13cm (length)

Add on seam allowance for height: 1cm
    (1cm + 4cm = 5cm)
Add on seam allowance for length: 2.5cm
    (2.5cm + 13cm = 15.5cm)

Size of Rectangle To Cut: 5 x 15.5cm

Using the 45° marking on the ruler, recut into a full trapezoid.
*See page 33 for cutting a full trapezoid.*

## TO CUT A LEFT OR RIGHT HALF TRAPEZOID

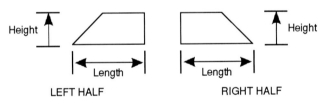

A left or right half trapezoid is cut from a rectangle.

Add 1cm to the height and 1.75cm to the length of the desired FINISHED size.

EXAMPLE:
Desired FINISHED height:
        5cm (height) x 15cm (length)

Add on seam allowance for height: 1cm
    (1cm + 5cm = 6cm)
Add on seam allowance for length: 1.75cm
    (1.75cm + 15cm = 16.75cm)

Size of Rectangle To Cut: 6 x 16.75cm
Using the 45° marking on the ruler, recut into a left or right half trapezoid.
*See page 35 for cutting a half trapezoid.*

## TO CUT A DOUBLE PRISM

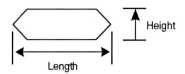

A double prism is cut from a rectangle.

Add 1/2" to the height and 3/4" to the length of the desired FINISHED size.

EXAMPLE:
Desired FINISHED size:
       2" (height) x 4 1/2" (length)

Add on seam allowance to the height: 1/2"
       (1/2" + 2" = 2 1/2")
Add on seam allowance to the length: 3/4"
       (3/4" + 4 1/2" = 5 1/4")

Size of Rectangle To Cut:  2 1/2" x 5 1/4"

Using the 45° markings on ruler, recut into a double prism.
*See page 38 for cutting a double prism.*

## TO CUT A DOUBLE PRISM

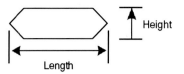

A double prism is cut from a rectangle.

Add 1cm to the height and 1.5cm to the length of the desired FINISHED size.

EXAMPLE:
Desired FINISHED size:
       5cm (height) x 12.5cm (length)

Add on seam allowance to the height: 1cm
       (1cm + 5cm = 6cm)
Add on seam allowance to the length: 1.5cm
       (1.5cm + 12.5cm = 14cm)

Size of Rectangle To Cut:  6 x 14cm

Using the 45° markings on  ruler, recut into a double prism.
*See page 38  for cutting a double prism.*

## TO CUT A PRISM

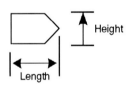

A prism is cut from a rectangle.

Add 1/2" to the height and 5/8" to the length of the desired FINISHED size.

EXAMPLE:
Desired FINISHED size:
       2" (height)  x 3" (length)

Add on seam allowance to the height: 1/2"
       (1/2" + 2 = 2 1/2")
Add on seam allowance to the length: 5/8"
       (5/8" + 3" = 3 5/8")

Size of Rectangle To Cut:  2 1/2" x 3 5/8"
Using the 45° markings on ruler, recut into a prism.
*See page 39 for cutting a prism.*

## TO CUT A PRISM

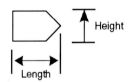

A prism is cut from a rectangle.

Add 1cm to the height and 1.25cm to the length of the desired FINISHED size.

EXAMPLE:
Desired FINISHED height:
       5cm (height) x 8cm (length)

Add on seam allowance to the height: 1cm
       (1cm + 5cm = 6cm)
Add on seam allowance to the length: 1.25cm
       (1.25cm + 8cm = 9.25cm)

Size of Rectangle To Cut:  6 x 9.25cm
Using the 45° markings on  ruler, recut into a prism.
*See page 39 for cutting a prism.*

## TO CUT A KITE SHAPE

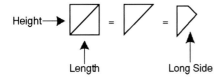

Height→     Length     Long Side

The kite shape is first cut from a square. The square is cut in half diagonally, then into a kite shape.

Add 7/8" to the desired FINISHED length of the long side of the kite shape.

EXAMPLE:
Desired FINISHED length of long side: 2"

Add on seam allowance: 7/8"
    (7/8" + 2" = 2 7/8")

Size of Square To Cut: 2 7/8" x 2 7/8"

Cut square in half diagonally.

*Follow the directions on page 36 to finish cutting the desired shape.*


## TO CUT A CLIPPED SQUARE

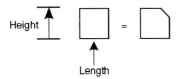

Height     Length

A clipped square is made from a square, with one of its corners cut off.

Add 1/2" to the height and 1/2" to the length of the desired FINISHED size.

To Find The Width Of The Diagonal Cut: After drawing the square on graph paper, determine how much of the square you want clipped off. Add 1/4" to the diagonal clip for seam allowance. Draw a diagonal line from corner to corner of the square. Measure from the diagonal line to the cutting line. Cut off the excess corner and discard.

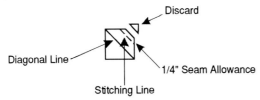

Discard
Diagonal Line
1/4" Seam Allowance
Stitching Line

*See page 39 for cutting how to.*

---

## TO CUT A KITE SHAPE

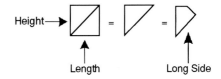

Height→     Length     Long Side

The kite shape is first cut from a square. The square is cut in half diagonally, then into a kite shape.

Add 1.75cm to the desired FINISHED length of the long side of the kite shape.

EXAMPLE:
Desired FINISHED length of long side: 5cm

Add on seam allowance: 1.75cm
    (1.75cm + 5cm = 6.75cm)

Size of Square To Cut: 6.75 x 6.75cm

Cut square in half diagonally.

*Follow the directions on page 36 to finish cutting the desired shape.*


## TO CUT A CLIPPED SQUARE

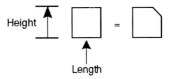

Height     Length

A clipped square is made from a square, with one of its corners cut off.

Add 1cm to the height and 1cm to the length of the desired FINISHED size.

To Find The Width Of The Diagonal Cut: After drawing the square on graph paper, determine how much of the square you want clipped off. Add 5mm to the diagonal clip for seam allowance. Draw a diagonal line from corner to corner of the square. Measure from the diagonal line to the cutting line. Cut off the excess corner and discard.

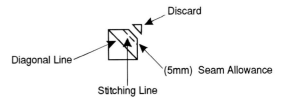

Discard
Diagonal Line
(5mm) Seam Allowance
Stitching Line

*See page 39 for cutting how to.*

# STEP TWO

## GETTING THE MOST FROM YOUR SEWING MACHINE

### NEEDLE SIZE

I always use a size 11 (Metric #75) needle in my machine. It is fine and sharp so it pierces instead of pushing through the fabric. Change your needle frequently. The cost of needles is small versus ruining your fabric or putting extra strain on your sewing machine. If you are getting small white pulls in your fabric while sewing, that is a sure sign of a dull needle. Change the needle immediately.

### PRESSER FOOT

Use an open toe or applique foot. This type of foot allows you to see where your needle is sewing at all times. This is especially important when you are setting in squares or triangles. (This method will be discussed later in the chapter). If you can't buy this type of foot for your machine, cut the bars off an existing foot. A fine tooth hacksaw and metal file are all you will need. Be careful and be sure to smooth down any burrs with the file.

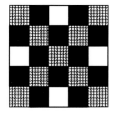

### GETTING AN ACCURATE 1/4" (5MM) SEAM ALLOWANCE

In order for your quilt blocks to be the right size, you must use the proper seam allowance. In quilt making this seam allowance is usually 1/4". Quilters who use the metric system should use 5mm, about 1/5". All of the metric patterns in this book have been developed using a 5mm seam allowance. Do not depend on your presser foot for the 1/4" (5mm) seam allowance. I learned the hard way that the edge of my presser foot was not a true 1/4" (5mm).

While working on my Double Irish Chain Quilt, I used the edge of my presser foot for my 1/4" guide. This was great until I tried to butt Block A to Block B. Block A was sewn with what I thought was a 1/4" seam allowance. Block B was a 10 1/2" square with an appliqued square in each corner. The four appliqued squares had been turned under 1/4".

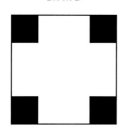

As you can see in the example, the appliqued squares appear larger than the squares in Block A. The overall block sizes were also different.

Block B was the correct size. In order to finish making the quilt, I had to trim some of the B Blocks and reapplique some of the corner squares. It's a wonder I ever stayed with quiltmaking!

*After a lot of trial and error, I finally developed a method that I have used for almost ten years. I would like to share this technique with you.*

*Position the point of the needle so it is ready to enter the hole in the throat plate. (Remember only the point of the needle. The needle diameter keeps getting larger the further up the needle you go).*

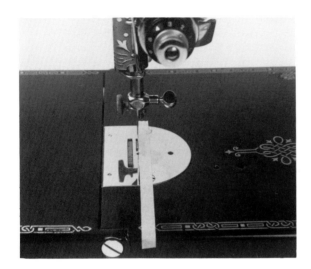

*Place a long piece of 1/4" tape parallel to the needle. The tape will be perpendicular to the long axis of the sewing machine.*

*Now place another piece of masking tape next to the first piece.*

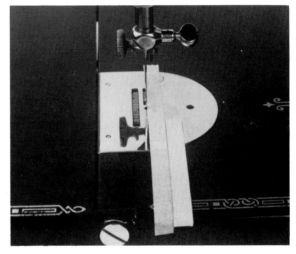

*Pull off the first piece of tape. The measurement from the point of the needle to the edge of the tape should be a 1/4". Metric quilters should use 5mm masking tape, or cut two 5mm wide strips from wider masking tape.*

*Don't take this for granted. Cut two pieces of fabric with your rotary cutter and ruler. Gently butt the fabric next to the tape and sew the length of the fabric. Place the ruler on top of the two sewn pieces and see if the 1/4" (5mm) marking on the ruler hides the stitching line.*

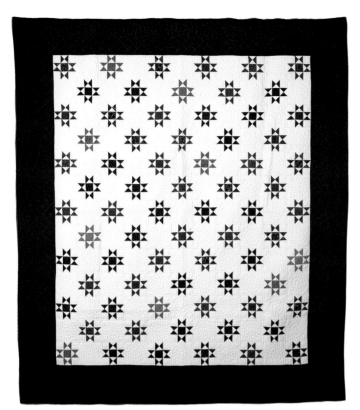

*Ohio Star from the collection of Jeanne and Gene Wilber - The Strawberry Patch Calico Shop*

*Thousand Pyramids from the collection of Jeanne and Gene Wilber - The Strawberry Patch Calico Shop*

If it does, you're in great shape. If not, you can easily correct this problem. If your seam allowance is too small, place the first piece of masking tape a hair to the right of the second piece of tape. Now remove the second piece of tape and butt it next to the first piece. Remove the first piece. Cut and sew a new sample and measure for the 1/4" (5mm) seam allowance.

If your seam allowance is too large, place the first piece of tape a hair to the left of the second piece of tape. Now remove the second piece of tape and butt it against the first piece. Remove the first piece. Cut and sew a new sample and measure for the 1/4" (5mm) seam allowance.

After you have located your 1/4" (5mm) seam allowance, place several (6-8) layers of 3/4" masking tape or filament tape over the 1/4" (5mm) tape. You want to create a high ridge or edge so you can butt your fabric against it.

I often come across sewing machines with front loading bobbin cases. This is no problem. After layering your tape, take a craft knife or put an old blade in your rotary cutter and cut the tape so you can get into your bobbin case. When you close the bobbin case, the two pieces of tape will still be in alignment. This method also works for free arm machines.

I occasionally get a few questions about using a scant 1/4" (5mm) seam allowance. My answer is this: You be the judge. Try sewing the Churn Dash pattern on page 60. See how close you come to having a 6 1/2" (15.2cm) unfinished block. To get a 6 1/2" (15.2cm) square you may have to adjust your seam allowance even though the ruler shows you are using a 1/4" (5mm) seam allowance. Again, you be the judge.

### SETTING IN SQUARES AND TRIANGLES

I have shared many of my secrets in the pages of this book, but the one I am going to write about now is especially important.

Do you love Eight Pointed Stars and Lone Star quilts but have difficulty when setting in the squares and triangles? Is the opening into which you are trying to set the square or triangle too big or too small? The reason for this is because you didn't stop sewing **1/4" (5mm)** from the end of the pieces.

Here's my secret for getting a perfect 1/4" (5mm) stop **every time**. Start sewing two 3" (7.6cm) squares together. Continue sewing until you come to what looks like 1/4" (5mm) from the end of the piece. Stop sewing with the needle half way into the fabric. (Do not catch the bobbin thread on the last stitch).

*Stitching is 1/4" from edge*

Now, lift the presser foot up and turn the fabric and see if it butts up against the tape you are using for your seam allowance. If it butts against the tape, you have a true 1/4" (5mm) stop!

Turn the fabric back as shown in the preceding photo and back tack. (To back tack, sew in reverse two or three stitches).

If your fabric doesn't butt up against the tape or the fabric goes over the tape, you do not have a perfect 1/4" (5mm) stop. You can easily fix this problem. Turn the handwheel so the needle comes out of the fabric without catching the bobbin thread. Carefully move the fabric either to the left or right until it butts against the tape. Once you find the right spot, turn the handwheel so the needle goes through the fabric and catches the bobbin thread. Turn the fabric back as shown in the photo on page 54 and back tack.

After using my technique, you will have perfect set in seams every time.

### PINNING

No matter how good your sewing machine is, sometimes it needs a helping hand. Here's where the proper type of pins can make or break your project.

After writing Miniature To Masterpiece©, I did a lot more research, finding a silk pin called IBC by Clotilde that works really well.

Not only is the IBC pin extra long, thin and sharp, but there are 500 pins in each box. They will also help you keep a 1/4" (5mm) seam allowance as you near the end of your piecing. Because of its length you are able to hold the head of the last pin to guide your fabric through.

I believe you should use a pin with the smallest head possible. You want your fabric to lie flat on the throat plate while sewing. This is not possible if you are using a pin with a large head.

If you have problems with the small headed silk pins, IBC also makes the same pin with a small glass head. These work well for people who have difficulty holding small objects.

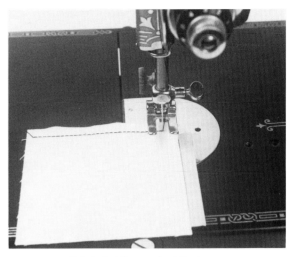
*Fabric butting against the tape - A perfect 1/4" (5mm) stop!*

*IBC Pin guiding the fabric through*

*Fine silk pins by IBC*

# STEP THREE

PRESSING

Once you have mastered accurate cutting and sewing, the last step is careful pressing . In my experience, it seems that a quilter's personality really comes out when she/he gets hold of an iron. Here are some of the personalities I have seen. **#1. *The Attack Personality* -** A person who thinks they are pressing their child's jeans instead of a quilt block. Yes, I know jeans are made of 100% cotton, but it is a different weight cotton than quilting cotton. You do not have to push down on the iron. It is the heat of the iron that does the job of pressing, not the hand pressure. I personally use a light weight iron because it is less stressful for my hands. I also discovered that irons with plastic-coated bottoms did not seem to heat as hot as the noncoated irons. Consequently, I don't use a plastic-coated iron. **#2. *The Steamer Personality*** - the quilter who sprays her block with water and then proceeds to steam it to death. Whenever I tried using steam, I noticed that it slightly stretched the block. It made the areas where the seams are butted together appear shiny looking. Plus, this area really tends to stand out, due to the compression of the fibers. It appears that the cause of this is spraying, using steam and pressing down hard on the iron. I guess by now you know I don't use steam! **#3. *Driving Backwards Personality* -** a person who always presses on the wrong side of the fabric. Remember my analogy in the rotary cutting chapter? Driving a car forward is a lot easier than backing up. The same comparison holds true in pressing. The only time I press on the wrong side is when I'm setting the seam. (You'll read more about this later). After setting the seam I **always** press on the right side of the fabric. You want to be able to see what's going on with the block, and the only way you can do this is to press on the right side. Students frequently comment to me, "After I get through pressing and turn the block over, I have to repress because I have pleats." (This is when the fabric is not entirely pressed smooth. Some of the fabric is tucked under the seam allowance). The reason for this is simple. You cannot see what is going on while pressing on the back side of the block.

I must admit to you that I have been all of these personalities! Through trial and a lot of error, I have finally developed a really good pressing system. In my first book, Miniature to Masterpiece©, I described some of my methods. Feedback from readers and fellow quilters, has prompted me to repeat and expand on these **critical** techniques in this book. Also, many people have asked for graphics or photos of my techniques. Since most of us learn much faster by seeing something done, I am happy to respond to this need. Remember, what you read in the pressing section is Food For Thought. Experiment **and** adapt these techniques if they work as well for you as they do for me.

### SETTING THE SEAM ALLOWANCE

After sewing you should press every seam **closed** before you press to the light or dark fabric. By doing this, you will ease in any puffiness caused by the machine tension. Any time my seam is longer than 2" (5mm), I set the seam. This is **imperative**. Also, **do not** press in an east to west (side to side) movement. Press in a north to south (up and down) movement while moving the iron along the strip. The photos below are of a right handed person setting the seam.

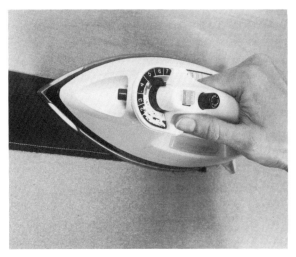

*Notice the iron is north above the seam allowance*

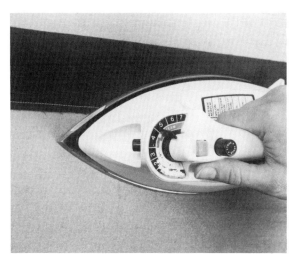

*Notice the iron is south of the seam allowance*

### PRESSING LONG SEAMS

I have found that if I don't set the seam, and press north to south, I will end up with a slightly **bowed** strip.

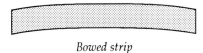

*Bowed strip*

Here is a practice test for you.

**Step One** - Sew two (1 light, 1 dark) - 2 1/2" x 22" (6.5 x 60cm) strips together.

**Step Two** - Place the strip, **wrong side,** on the ironing board with the seam allowance **facing** your body. It is **important** that the seam allowance always faces your body. Your hands have a natural tendency to work towards you, not away from you.

Set the seam by pressing north to south while moving the iron. See photos above.

**Step Three** - Without lifting the strip, gently separate the two layers of fabric so you are looking at the **right side**. Starting in the **middle** of the strip, place your four fingers on top of the seam line and your thumb **underneath** the fabric.

*Four fingers slightly ahead of the iron*
*Thumb is underneath the fabric*

Start pressing in a north to south movement until you come to the end of the strip. Your four fingers will be doing a slight finger press just ahead of the iron; while your thumb will make sure the seam allowance is towards your body. Also, by having your fingers ahead of the iron, they will prevent any pleats from forming.

**Step Four** - Go back to the beginning of the strip. Now you will start pressing **3" in from the end of the strip**. (By starting to press 3" in from the end of the strip, you will avoid creating a bowed strip.) Place your four fingers on top of the seam line and your thumb **underneath** the fabric. Start pressing in a north to south movement until you connect with the middle pressed area.

**Step Five** - Go back to the 3" unpressed area. Finger press and then set the iron on this section. You need not move the iron around. Now you will have a perfectly pressed straight strip.

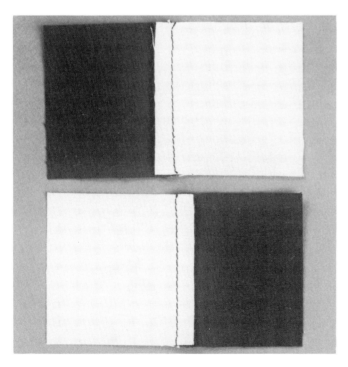

*One seam pressed to the west*
*One seam pressed to the east*

### BUTTING THE SEAMS

In quiltmaking it is much easier to keep your blocks square if you butt your seams together as often as possible. This means that one of the seam allowances is pressed so it will be facing one way, and the other seam allowance is pressed so it will be facing the opposite way.

You will notice in the pattern section, I have included the pressing directions for all the blocks.

# CHOOSING A PATTERN

### No Templates

You will find 51 patterns in this book. I chose these patterns from hundreds I have made because I want each of you to experience the joy of total rotary cutting while using no templates. In each pattern you will note that I state the seam allowance used. Also I identify each shape and tell you what page you can find the cutting directions on. Lastly, you will notice I have included complete pressing directions.

### Using Templates

Even though the patterns were designed without the use of templates, you can easily make templates for each piece if you desire to. I will use the 6" (15.2cm) Ohio Star on page 77 for this example.

### Shape A, B and C

Shape A, B and C are the same shape, so you will only need one template. Draw a 3 1/4" (7.6cm) square on your template material. Draw a line diagonally from corner to corner. Now draw another line diagonally from the other opposite corners. You will now be able to see four triangles within the square. With your ruler and cutter, only cut out one of the triangles. You will use this one template to cut all the A, B and C pieces. Mark the appropriate number and color you need for each piece on the template.

### Shape D and E

Shape D and E are the same size. You only need to draw one 2 1/2" (6.1cm) square. Cut out the square with your ruler and cutter. Mark the template with the appropriate colors and how many pieces you need of each color.

I can not stress how important it is to be cutting your templates with your ruler and cutter, not scissors. You will loose accuracy if you use scissors, it's that simple! The only time I use scissors to cut templates is when the template has a curve.

### The Best Part

It doesn't matter if you want to totally rotary cut your pieces or cut templates to the patterns. The seam allowance for **each** piece is **already** included. I have taken the guess-work out of these patterns.

# CHURN DASH

Block Size: 6" (15.2cm) square finished
Seam allowance: 1/4" (5mm)

Shapes Used In This Pattern and How To Cut Them:

Shape A, B - Half Square Triangle - Page 17

Shape C, D - Rectangle - Page 18

Shape E - Square - Page 16

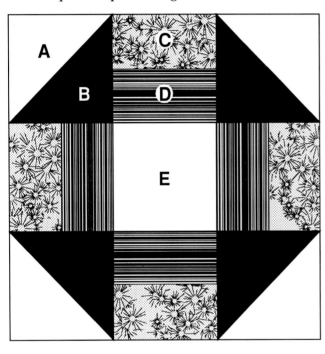

## CUTTING PROCEDURE:

A - Cut 2 - 2 7/8" (6.8cm) squares, light. Cut in half diagonally.

B - Cut 2 - 2 7/8" (6.8cm) squares, dark. Cut in half diagonally.

C - Cut 1 - 1 1/2" x 12" (3.5 x 30.2cm) strip, medium light.

D - Cut 1 - 1 1/2" x 12" ( 3.5 x 30.2cm) strip, medium dark.

E - Cut 1 - 2 1/2" (6.1cm) square, light.

## SEWING PROCEDURE:

1. Sew A to B. Press to B. Make four squares.

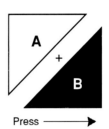

Press ⟶

2. Sew C strip to D strip. Press to D. Recut into four 2 1/2" (6.1cm) pieces. Discard the excess.

2 1/2" (6.1cm)

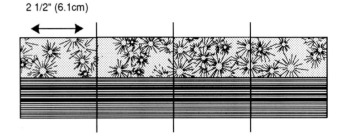

3. Pin and sew into rows. Press according to the diagram.

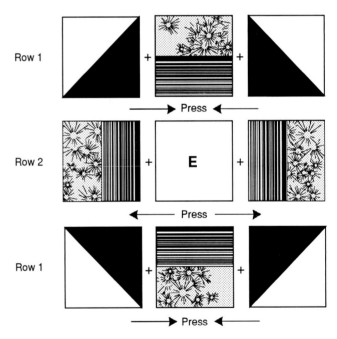

4. Butt, pin and sew the rows together. Press Row 1 towards Row 2.

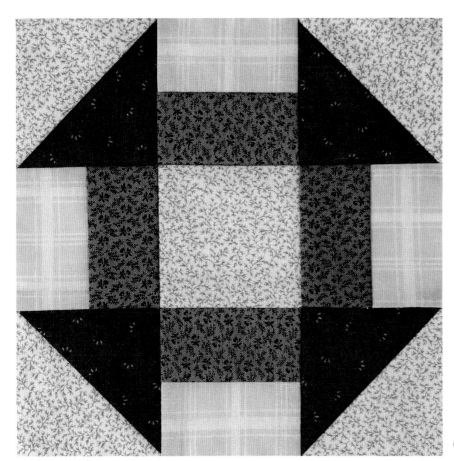

*Churn Dash*

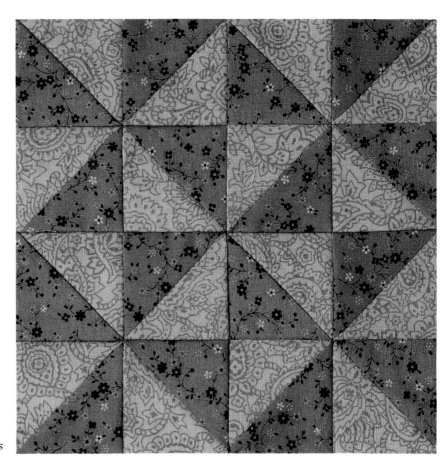

*Double Pinwheels*

# DOUBLE PINWHEELS

Block size: 6" (15.2cm) square finished
Seam allowance: 1/4" (5mm)

Shapes Used In This Pattern and How To Cut Them:

Shape - A,B - Half Square Triangle - Page 17

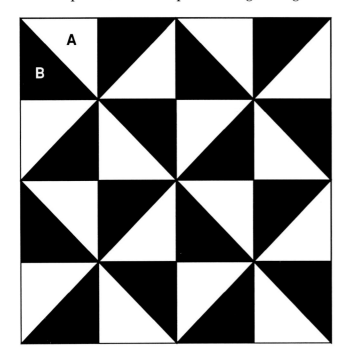

## CUTTING PROCEDURE:

A -  Cut 8 - 2 3/8" (5.6cm) squares, light. Cut in half diagonally.

B -  Cut 8 - 2 3/8" (5.6cm) squares, dark. Cut in half diagonally.

## SEWING PROCEDURE:

1. Sew A to B to make a square. Press to B. Make sixteen squares.

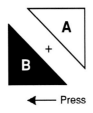

2. Sew two squares together. Press to B. Make eight sets.

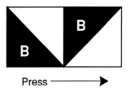

3. Butt, pin and sew two sets together. It doesn't matter which way you press the center seam. Make four pinwheels.

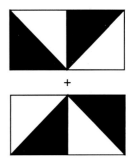

4. Butt, pin and sew into rows. (Make sure the center seam is facing up on one of the pinwheels and facing down on the other pinwheel). Press according to the diagram.

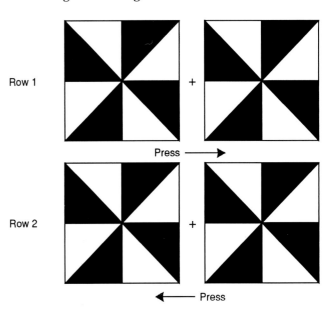

5. Butt, pin and sew the rows together. Press Row 1 towards Row 2.

# DOUBLE SQUARES

Block Size: 6" (15.2cm) square finished
Seam allowance: 1/4" (5mm)

Shapes Used In This Pattern and How To Cut Them:

    Shape A,B,C,D - Half Square Triangle - Page 17

    Shape E - Full Trapezoid - Page 33

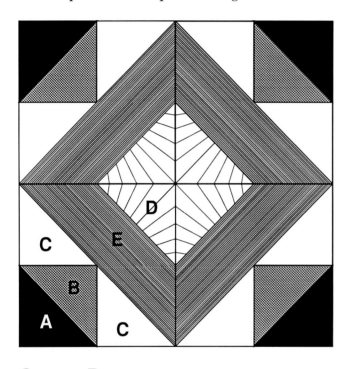

## CUTTING PROCEDURE:

A - Cut 2 - 2 3/8" (5.6cm) squares, dark. Cut in half diagonally.

B - Cut 2 - 2 3/8" (5.6cm) squares, medium dark. Cut in half diagonally.

C - Cut 4 - 2 3/8" (5.6cm) squares, light. Cut in half diagonally.

D - Cut 2 - 2 3/8" (5.6cm) squares, medium light. Cut in half diagonally.

E - Cut 4 - 1 5/8" x 5 1/2" (3.9 x 13.3cm) rectangles, medium dark. Cut each into a full trapezoid.

## SEWING PROCEDURE:

1. Sew A to B. Press to A. Make four squares.

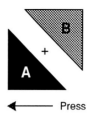
← Press

2. Sew C to the proper side of the square. Press to C. Sew another C to the other side of the square. Press to C. Make four sets.

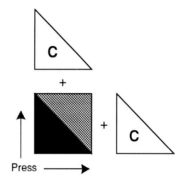

Press →

3. Sew D to E. Press to E. Make four sets.

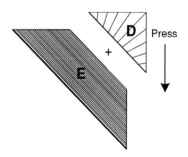

4. Sew the ABC set to the DE set. Press to DE. Make four units.

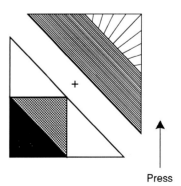

Press

5. Carefully pin and sew into rows. Press accord-ing to the diagram.

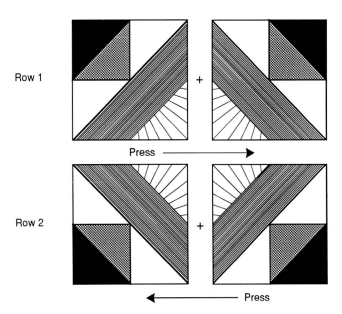

Row 1

Press ———————▶

Row 2

◀——————— Press

6. Carefully pin and sew rows together. Press Row 1 towards Row 2.

# DUTCHMAN'S PUZZLE

Block Size: 6" (15.2cm) square finished
Seam allowance: 1/4" (5mm)

Shapes Used In This Pattern and How To Cut Them:

    Shape A,B - Quarter Square Triangle - Page 18

    Shape C,D - Half Square Triangle - Page 17

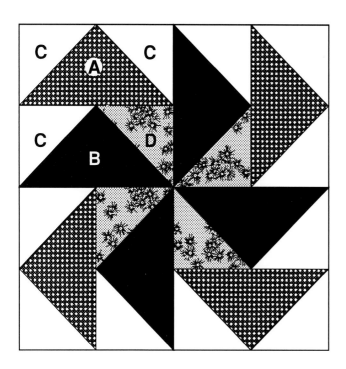

## CUTTING PROCEDURE:

A - Cut 1 - 4 1/4" (10.1cm) square, medium dark. Cut in half diagonally twice.

B - Cut 1 - 4 1/4" (10.1cm) square, dark. Cut in half diagonally twice.

C - Cut 6 - 2 1/2" (5.9cm) squares, light. Cut in half diagonally. These pieces are slightly oversized.

D - Cut 2 - 2 1/2" (5.9cm) squares, medium light. Cut in half diagonally. These pieces are slightly oversized.

## SEWING PROCEDURE:

1. Sew one C to the side of A. Press to C. Sew another C to the other side of A. Press to C. Cut off all dog ears. Make four sets.

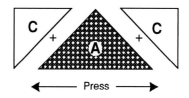

2. Sew one C to the side of B. Press to C. Sew one D to the other side of B. Press to D. Cut off all dog ears. Make four sets.

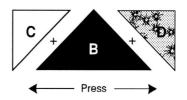

3. After sewing and pressing, trim the top of the block to within 1/4" (5mm) of the goose. Your geese should measure 2" x 3 1/2" (4.8 x 8.6cm).

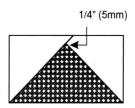

4. Sew the geese together in the proper order. Press to the A goose. Make four units.

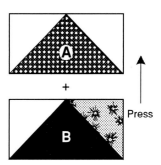

5. Butt, pin and sew into rows. Press according to the diagram.

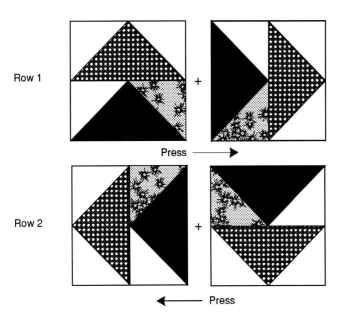

Row 1

Press ⟶

Row 2

⟵ Press

6. Butt, pin and sew rows together. Press Row 1 towards Row 2.

# FLOWER BASKET

Block Size: 6" (15.2cm) square finished
Seam allowance: 1/4" (5mm)

Shapes Used In This Pattern and How To Cut Them:

    A,B,C,E,F - Half Square Triangle - Page 17

    D - Rectangle - Page 18

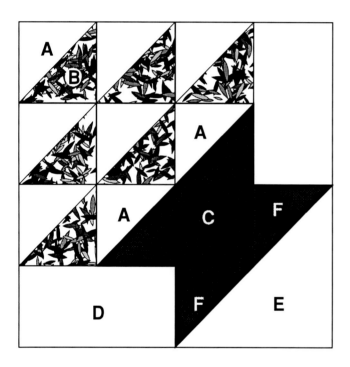

## CUTTING PROCEDURE:

A - Cut 4 - 2 3/8" (5.6cm) squares, light. Cut in half diagonally.

B - Cut 3 - 2 3/8" (5.6cm) squares, medium dark. Cut in half diagonally.

C - Cut 1 - 3 7/8" (9.4cm) square, dark. Cut in half diagonally. You will only use one triangle.

D - Cut 2 - 2" x 3 1/2" (4.8 x 8.6cm) rectangles, light.

E - Cut 1 - 3 7/8" (9.4cm) square, light. Cut in half diagonally. You will only use one triangle.

F - Cut 1 - 2 3/8" (5.6cm) square, dark. Cut in half diagonally.

## SEWING PROCEDURE:

1. Sew A to B. Press to B. Make six squares.

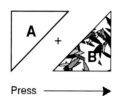

2. Row 1: Sew three squares together. Press according to the diagram.

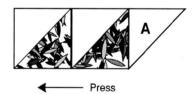

3. Row 2: Sew two squares and one A triangle together. Press according to the diagram.

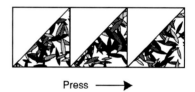

4. Row 3: Sew one square and one A triangle together. Press according to the diagram.

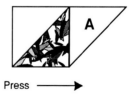

5. Butt, pin and sew the rows together. Press towards Row 3.

6. Sew C triangle to the sewn AB rows. Press to C.

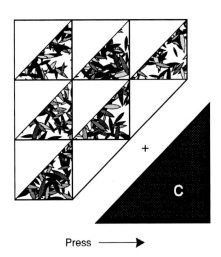

Press ——————▶

7. Sew a F triangle to D. Press to D. F triangle tip will hang over slightly. Do not trim. (You will use these tips when adding on E piece).

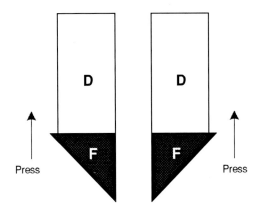

Press ↑          ↑ Press

8. Sew the DF piece to the proper sides. Press to DF piece.

Press ——————▶

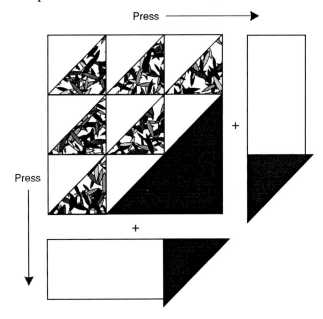

Press ↓          +          +

9. Sew E to the basket. Note: F triangle tips will line up with the two tips of E triangle. Press to E.

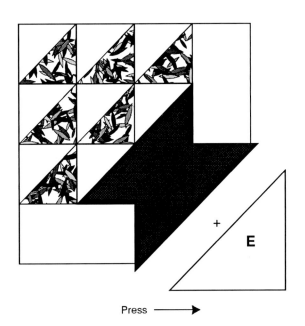

Press ——————▶

# HOME TREASURE

Block Size: 6" (15.2cm) square finished
Seam allowance: 1/4" (5mm)

Shapes Used In This Pattern and How To Cut Them:

Shape A - Square - Page 16

Shape B, F,H - Half Square Triangle - Page 17

Shape C,D, G - Rectangle - Page 18

Shape E - Prism - Page 39

## CUTTING PROCEDURE:

A - Cut 1 - 2" (4.8 cm) square, medium dark.

B - Cut 2 - 2" (4.6cm) squares, light. Cut in half diagonally.

C - Cut 4 - 1 1/4" x 2 5/8" (2.9 x 6.4 cm) rectangles, dark.

D - Cut 4 - 1 1/4" x 2 5/8" (2.9 x 6.4 cm) rectangles, light.

E - Cut 1 - 2 3/8" x 12" (5.8 x 30.1 cm) strip, dark. Cut into four 2 5/8" (6.3 cm) pieces. Recut each into the prism shape. (Recut the 2 5/8" (6.3cm) side, not the 2 3/8" (5.8cm).

F - Cut 4 - 1 5/8" (3.7cm) squares, light. Recut in half diagonally.

G - Cut 4 - 1 1/4" x 2" (2.9 x 4.8 cm) rectangles, medium dark.

H - Cut 2 - 1 7/8" (4.3 cm) squares, light. Recut in half diagonally.

## SEWING PROCEDURE:

1. Sew one B piece to the opposite sides of A. Press to B. Sew one B piece to the top and bottom of A. Press to B.

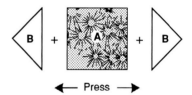

2. Sew F to each side of G. Press to F. Make four sets.

3. Sew H to the top of the FG pieces. Press to H. Make four sets.

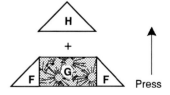

4. Sew C to D. Add E. Press seams toward E. Make four sets.

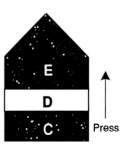

5. Side Unit: Sew one FGH set to each side of the CDE set. Press to the CDE set. Make two units.

6. Center Unit: Sew center AB square to the remaining CDE sets. Press to CDE unit.

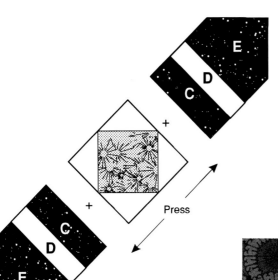

7. Butt, pin and sew the side units to the center unit. Press to the center unit.

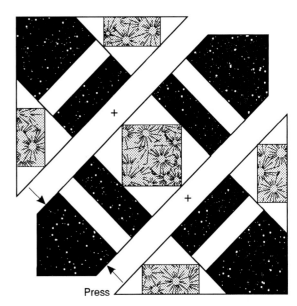

# MELON PATCH

Block Size: 6" (15.2cm) square finished
Seam allowance: 1/4" (5mm)

Shapes Used In This Pattern and How To Cut Them:

Shape A - Octagon - Page 28

Shape B - Half Square Triangle - Page 17

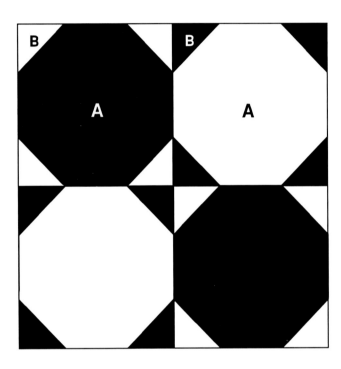

## CUTTING PROCEDURE:

A - Cut 2 - 3 1/2" (8.6cm) squares, dark. Recut into two octagons.

A - Cut 2 - 3 1/2" (8.6cm) squares, light. Recut into two octagons.

B - Cut 4 - 1 3/4" (4cm) squares, dark. Cut in half diagonally.

B - Cut 4 - 1 3/4" (4cm) squares, light. Cut in half diagonally.

## SEWING PROCEDURE:

1. Sew dark B to the proper corners of light A. Press to B. Make two sets.

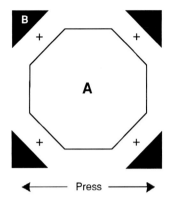

2. Sew light B to the proper corners of dark A. Press to A. Make two sets.

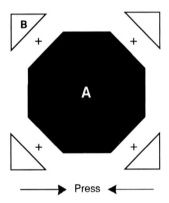

3. Butt, pin and sew into rows. Press according to the diagram.

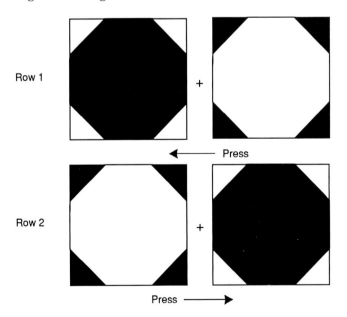

4. Butt, pin and sew the rows together. Press Row 1 towards Row 2.

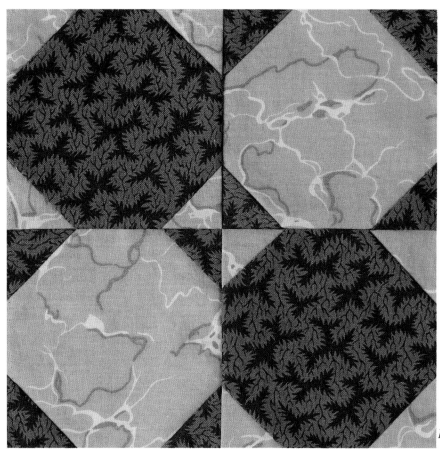

Melon Patch

Nelson's Victory

# NELSON'S VICTORY

Block size: 6" (15.2cm) square finished
Seam allowance: 1/4" (5mm)

Shapes Used In This Pattern and How To Cut Them:

Shape A - Left Half Trapezoid - Page 35

Shape B - Right Half Trapezoid - Page 35

Shape C - Square - Page 16

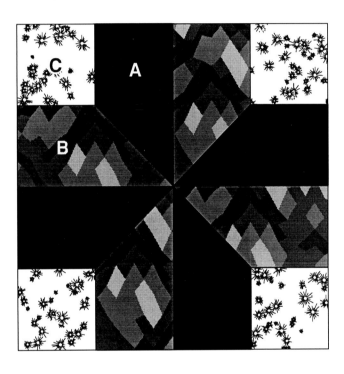

## CUTTING PROCEDURE:

A - Cut 4 - 2" x 3 7/8" (4.8 x9.4cm) rectangles, dark. Left hand quilters cut with the right side of the fabric facing you. Right hand quilters cut with the wrong side of the fabric facing you. Recut into four left half trapezoids.

B - Cut 4 - 2" x 3 7/8" (4.8 x 9.4cm) rectangles, medium dark. Left hand quilters cut with the wrong side of the fabric facing you. Right hand quilters cut with the right side of the fabric facing you. Recut into four right half trapezoids.

C - Cut 4 - 2" (4.8cm) squares, light.

## SEWING PROCEDURE:

1. Position A and B fabric right sides together. With the wrong side of B facing you, start sewing. Stop sewing 1/4" (5mm) from the edge and back tack. Do not press. Make four sets.

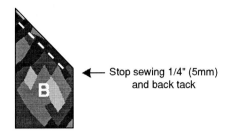

2. Pin the correct side of C to A. With the wrong side of A facing you, start sewing. Stop sewing when you reach the other seam and back tack. Cut the thread and remove from the machine.

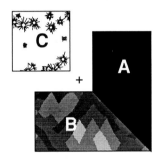

3. Pin the other side of C to B. With the wrong side of C facing you, start sewing. Stop sewing when you reach the other seam and back tack. Press to the AB section. Make four sets.

4. Butt, pin and sew into rows. Press according to the diagram.

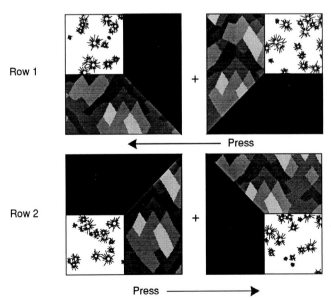

5. Butt, pin and sew rows together. Press Row 1 towards Row 2.

# NONESUCH

Block Size: 6" (15.2cm) square finished
Seam allowance: 1/4" (5mm)

Shapes Used In This Pattern and How To Cut Them:

    Shape A - Double Prism - Page 38

    Shape B,C - Half Square Triangle - Page 17

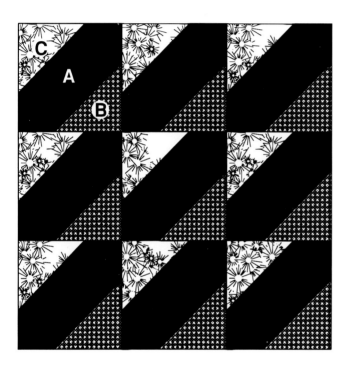

## CUTTING PROCEDURE:

A - Cut 9 - 1 5/8" x 3 5/8" (3.9 x 8.8) rectangles, dark. Recut each into a double prism shape.

B - Cut 5 - 2 1/8" (4.9cm) squares, medium dark. Cut in half diagonally. You will only use 9 triangles.

C - Cut 5 - 2 1/8" (4.9cm) squares, light. Cut in half diagonally. You will only use 9 triangles.

## SEWING PROCEDURE:

1. Sew A to B. Press to A. Add C. Press to A. Make nine blocks.

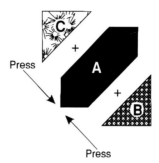

2. Pin and sew into rows. Press according to the diagram.

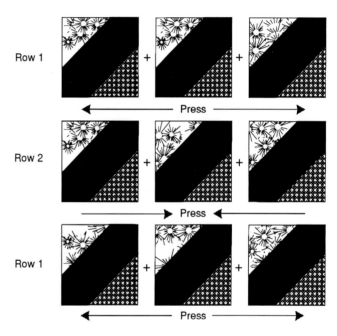

3. Butt, pin and sew rows together. It doesn't matter which way you press these seams.

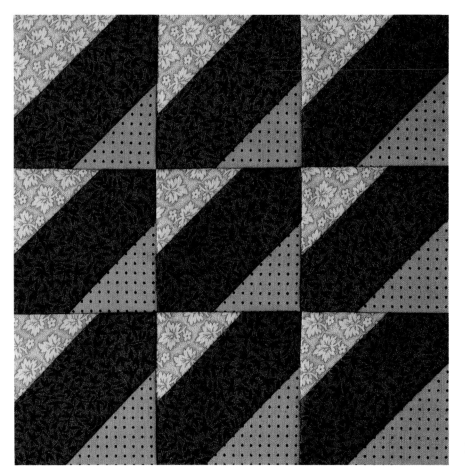

*Nonesuch*

*Ohio Star*

# OHIO STAR

Block size: 6" (15.2cm) square finished
Seam allowance: 1/4" (5mm)

Shapes Used In This Pattern and How To Cut Them:

Shape A,B,C - Quarter Square Triangle - Page 18

Shape D,E - Square - Page 16

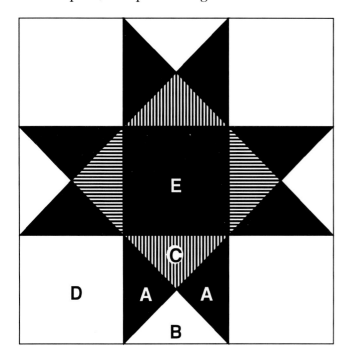

## CUTTING PROCEDURE:

A - Cut 2 - 3 1/4" (7.6cm) squares, dark.
Cut in half diagonally twice.

B - Cut 1 - 3 1/4" (7.6cm) square, light.
Cut in half diagonally twice.

C - Cut 1 - 3 1/4" (7.6cm) square, medium
light. Cut in half diagonally twice.

D - Cut 4 - 2 1/2" (6.1cm) squares, light.

E - Cut 1 - 2 1/2" (6.1cm) square, dark.

## SEWING PROCEDURE:

1. Sew A to B. Press to A. Make four sets.

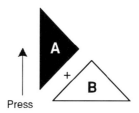

2. Sew A to C. Press to A. Make four sets.

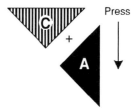

3. Butt, pin and sew the AB set to the AC set. Press to the AC set. Make four units.

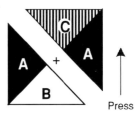

4. Pin and sew into rows. Press according to the diagram.

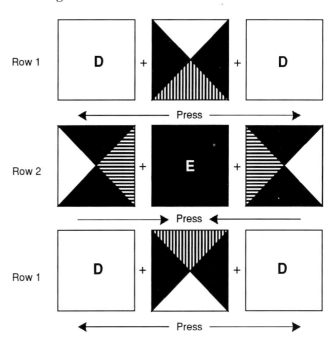

# THE CAT'S CRADLE

Block Size: 6" (15.2cm) square finished
Seam allowance: 1/4" (5mm)

Shapes Used In This Pattern and How To Cut Them:

Shape A - Square - Page 16

Shape B,C,D - Half Square Triangle - Page 17

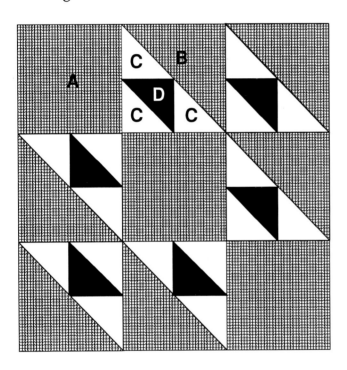

## CUTTING PROCEDURE:

A - Cut 3 - 2 1/2" (6.1cm) squares, medium light.

B - Cut 3 - 2 7/8" (6.8cm) squares, medium light. Cut in half diagonally.

C - Cut 9 - 1 7/8" (4.3cm) squares, light. Cut in half diagonally.

D - Cut 3 - 1 7/8" (4.3cm) squares, dark. Cut in half diagonally.

## SEWING PROCEDURE:

1. Sew C to D. Press to the dark. Make six squares.

2. Sew one C to each side of the CD square. Make six sets.

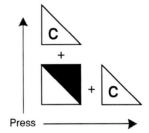

3. Sew B to the CD set. Make six units.

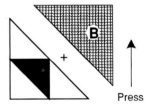

4. Pin and sew into rows. Press according to the diagram.

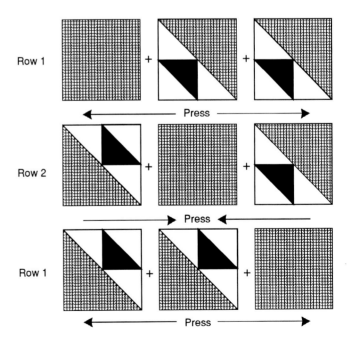

5. Butt, pin and sew rows together. Press Row 1 towards Row 2.

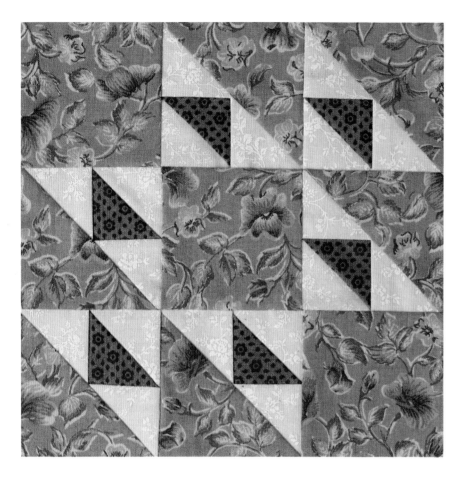

*The Cat's Cradle*

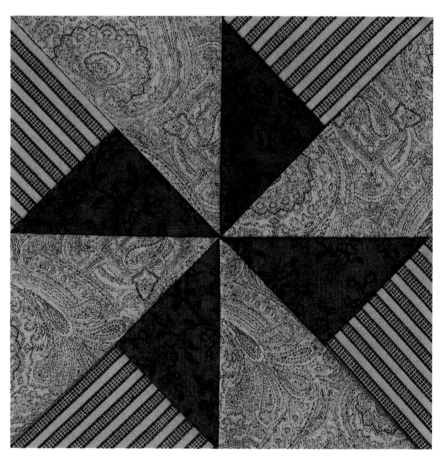

# WINDMILL

Block Size:  6" (15.2cm) square finished
Seam allowance:  1/4" (5mm)

Shapes Used In This Pattern and How To Cut Them:

Shape A - Half Square Triangle - Page 17

Shape B,C - Quarter Square Triangle - Page 18

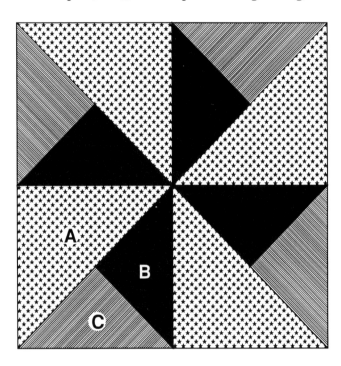

## CUTTING PROCEDURE:

A -  Cut 2 - 3 7/8" (9.4cm) squares, light. Cut in half diagonally.

B -  Cut 1 - 4 1/4" (10.1cm) square, dark. Cut in half diagonally twice.

C -  Cut 1 - 4 1/4" (10.1cm) square, medium light. Cut in half diagonally twice.

## SEWING PROCEDURE:

1. Sew B to C.  Press to B.  Make four sets.

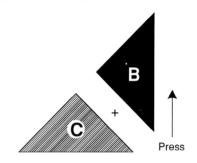

2. Sew a BC set to A.  Press to A.  Make four sets.

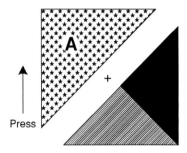

3. Butt, pin and sew into rows.  Press according to the diagram.

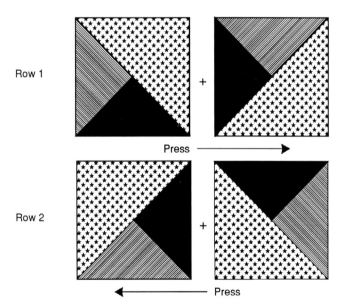

4. Butt, pin and sew the rows together.  Press Row 1 towards Row 2.

# BOW TIE

Block Size:  8" (20.3cm) square finished
Seam allowance:  1/4" (5mm)

Shapes Used In This Pattern and How To Cut Them:

    Shape A - Clipped Square - Page 39

    Shape B - Half Square Triangle - Page 17

    Shape C - Square - Page 16

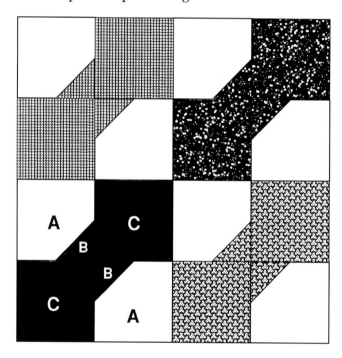

## CUTTING PROCEDURE FOR ONE BOW TIE BLOCK:

A - Cut 2 - 2 1/2" (6.1cm) squares, light. Position the ruler so the 1" (2.5cm) mark runs diagonally (corner to corner) on the square.  Cut off the excess tip.

Left Handed        Right Handed
1" (2.5cm)         1" (2.5cm)

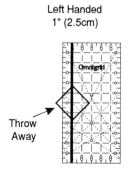
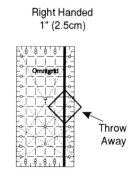

Throw Away        Throw Away

B - Cut 1 - 1 7/8" (4.3cm) square, dark. Cut in half diagonally.

C - Cut 2 - 2 1/2" (6.1cm) squares, dark.

## SEWING PROCEDURE FOR ONE BOW TIE BLOCK:

1. Sew A to B.  Press to B.  Square up B slightly if necessary.  Make two sets.

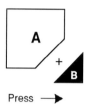

Press →

2. Sew an AB block to C.  Press to C.  Make two units.

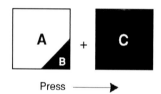

Press →

3. Sew ABC unit to other ABC unit.  Press.

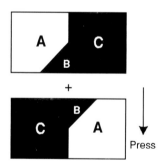

Use steps 1 through 3 to make three more Bow Tie blocks.

4. Turn the blocks so the center seam is facing up on one and down on the other. This will allow you to butt the blocks together. Sew into two rows. Sew the rows together. It doesn't matter which way you press the center seam.

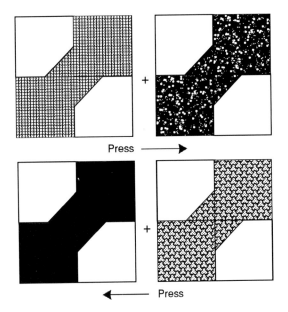

Press ⟶

Press ⟵

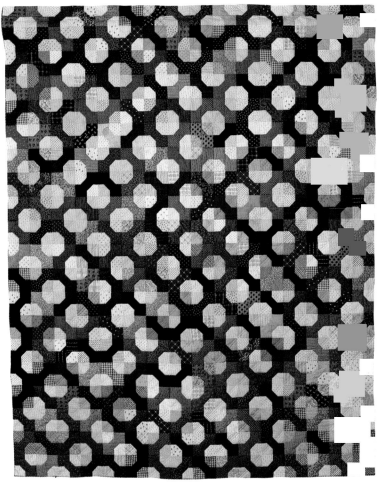

*Bow Tie Quilt made by*
*Carol Smith, Plains, Pa.*

# CRAZY ANN

Block Size: 8" (20.3cm) square finished
Seam allowance: 1/4" (5mm)

Shapes Used In This Pattern and How To Cut Them:

Shape A - Square  - Page 16

Shape B,C,E - Half Square Triangle - Page 17

Shape D,F - Quarter Square Triangle - Page 18

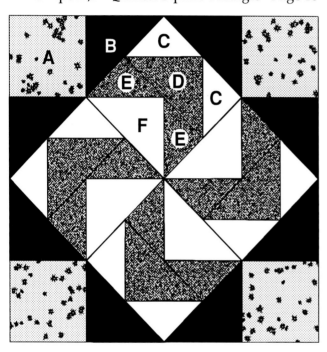

## CUTTING PROCEDURE:

A - Cut 4 - 2 1/2" (6.1cm) squares, medium light.

B - Cut 4 - 2 7/8" (6.8cm) squares, dark. Cut in half diagonally.

C - Cut 4 - 2 3/8" (5.6cm) squares, light. Cut in half diagonally.

D - Cut 1 - 4 1/8" (9.8cm) square, medium dark. Cut in half diagonally twice.

E - Cut 4 - 2 3/8" (5.6cm) squares, medium dark. Cut in half diagonally.

F - Cut 1 - 4 1/8" (9.8cm) square, light. Cut in half diagonally twice.

## SEWING PROCEDURE FOR THE CENTER BLOCK:

1. Sew one C to D. Press to C. Add another C to the other side of D. Press to C. Make four sets.

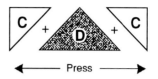

2. Sew one E to F. Press to E. Add another E to the other side of F. Press to E. Make four sets.

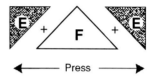

3. Sew a CD set to an EF set. Make four units. Press to the CD set.

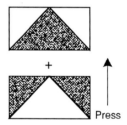

4. Butt, pin and sew into rows. Press according to the diagram.

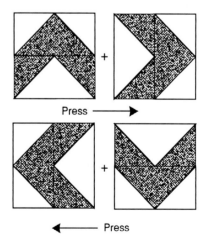

It doesn't matter which way you press the center seam.

## Sewing Procedure For The Corner Blocks:

5. Sew one B to the side of A. Press to A. Add another B to the other side of A. Press to A. Make four sets. By pressing to A, you will be able to easily butt this section to the center section.

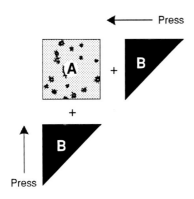

6. Sew a corner unit to opposite sides of the center block. Press to the AB blocks. Sew the remaining two corner units to the block. Press to the AB blocks.

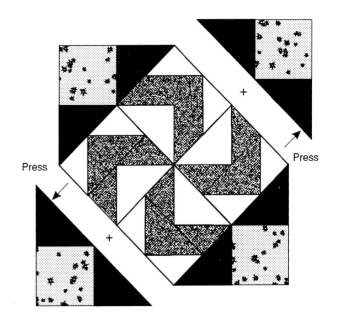

# DELECTABLE MOUNTAINS

Block Size: 8" (20.3cm) square finished
Seam allowance: 1/4" (5mm)

Shapes Used In This Pattern and How To Cut Them:

Shape A,B,E - Half Square Triangle - Page 17

Shape C,F - Square - Page 16

Shape D - Quarter Square Triangle - Page 18

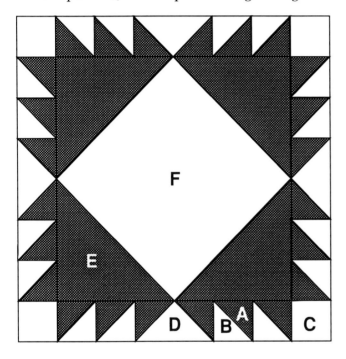

## CUTTING PROCEDURE:

A - Cut 1 - 1 7/8" x 24" (4.3 x 61cm) strip, dark. Cut into twelve 1 7/8" (4.3cm) squares. Recut in half diagonally.

B - Cut 1 - 1 7/8" x 17" (4.3 x 43.2cm) strip, light. Cut into eight 1 7/8" (4.3cm) squares. Recut in half diagonally.

C - Cut 4 - 1 1/2" (3.5cm) squares, light.

D - Cut 1 - 3 1/4" (7.6cm) square, light. Cut in half diagonally twice.

E - Cut 2 - 3 7/8" (9.4cm) squares, dark. Cut in half diagonally.

F - Cut 1 - 4 3/4" (11.8cm) square, light.

## SEWING PROCEDURE:

1. Sew A to B. Press to A. Make sixteen sets.

2. Sew one A to the side of D. Press to A. Sew another A to the other side of D. Press to A. Cut off dog ears. Make four sets.

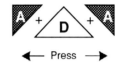

3. Sew two AB squares to each side of the AD piece. See diagram. Press away from the AD piece. Make four rows.

4. Add a C square to each end of two of the ABD rows. Press to C.

5. Sew E to the opposite sides of F. Press to F. (E will appear too big, but it is not). Sew the remaining two Es to the EF piece. Press to F. By pressing to F, you will be able to butt this unit with the AD unit.

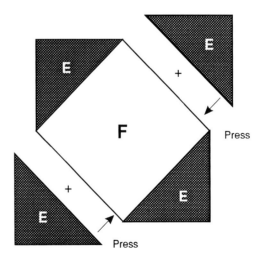

6. Sew an ABD row to each side of the EF square. Press to EF.

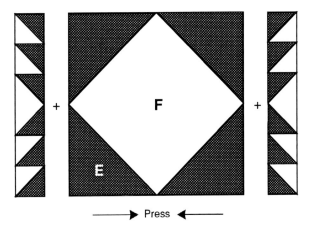

7. Butt, pin and sew an ABCD row to the top and bottom. Press towards the center square.

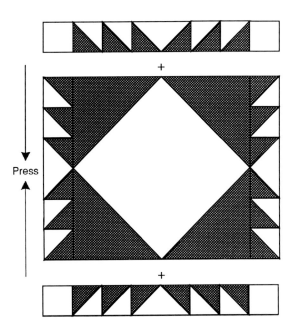

NOTE: *The hand tatted motif sewn in the center of my Delectable Mountains block was made by a friend, Marie Taylor, Williamsville, NY.*

# KENTUCKY CHAIN

Block Size: 8" (20.3cm) square finished
Seam allowance: 1/4" (5mm)

Shapes Used In This Pattern and How To Cut Them:

Shape A - Quarter Square Triangle - Page 18

Shape B - Prism - Page 39

Shape C - Double Prism - Page 38

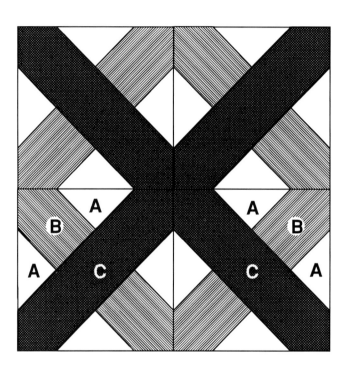

## CUTTING PROCEDURE:

A - Cut 4 - 3 1/2" (8.2cm) squares, light. Cut in half diagonally twice.

B - Cut 8 - 1 3/4" x 2 7/8" (4.2 x 7cm) rectangles, medium dark. Cut each into a prism shape.

C - Cut 4 - 1 3/4" x 6 1/2" (4.2 x 16.1cm) rectangles, dark. Cut each into a double prism shape.

## SEWING PROCEDURE:

1. Block A

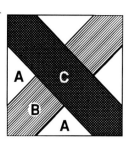

Sew A to each side of B. Press to B. Make four sets.

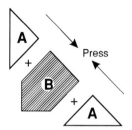

2. Sew one AB set to each side of C. Press to the AB set. Cut dog ears off. Make two units.

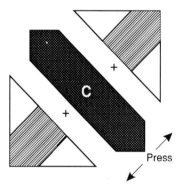

3. Block B

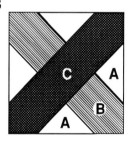

Sew A to each side of B. Press to A. Cut dog ears off. Make four sets.

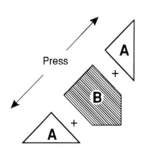

4. Sew one AB set to each side of C. Press to C. Make two units.

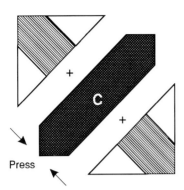

Press

NOTE: *By pressing the seams in the direction shown, you will be able to butt all the seams together when sewing the four blocks together.*

5. Butt, pin and sew into rows according to the diagram. Press to block A.

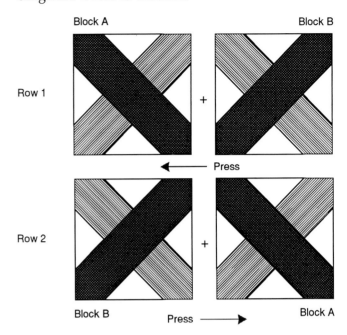

Block A                    Block B

Row 1                +

← Press

Row 2                +

Block B      Press →      Block A

6. Butt, pin and sew rows together. Press Row 1 towards Row 2.

# RISING STAR

Block Size:  8" (20.3cm) square finished
Seam allowance:  1/4" (5mm)

Shapes Used In This Pattern and How To Cut Them:

    Shape A,D,G - Square  - Page 16

    Shape B,E, - Half Square Triangle - Page 17

    Shape C,F - Quarter Square Triangle - Page 18

## CUTTING PROCEDURE:

A -  Cut 4 - 2 1/2" (6.1cm) squares, medium light.

B -  Cut 4 - 2 7/8" (6.8cm) squares, dark. Cut in half diagonally.

C -  Cut 1 - 5 1/4" (12.7cm) square, medium light. Cut in half diagonally twice.

D -  Cut 4 - 1 1/2" (3.5cm) squares, light.

E -  Cut 4 - 1 7/8" (4.3cm) squares, medium dark.  Cut in half diagonally.

F -  Cut 1 - 3 1/4" (7.6cm) square, light.  Cut in half diagonally twice.

G -  Cut 1 - 2 1/2" (6.1cm) square, medium dark.

## SEWING PROCEDURE FOR THE SMALL STAR:

1. Sew one E to F.  Press to E.  Add another E to the other side of F.  Press to E.  Make four sets.

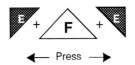

2. Pin and sew into rows.  Press according to the diagram.

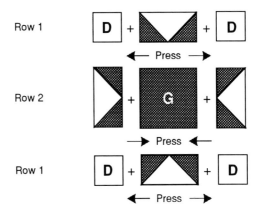

3. Butt, pin and sew rows together. Press Row 2 towards Row 1.

## SEWING PROCEDURE FOR THE LARGE STAR:

4. Sew one B to C.  Press to B.  Add another B to the other side of C.  Press to B.  Make four sets.

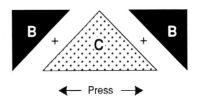

5. Pin and sew into rows. Press according to the diagram.

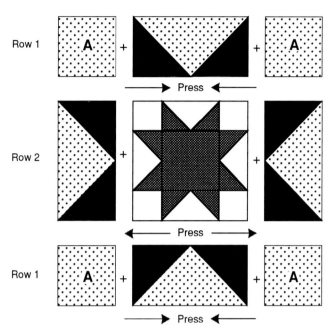

Row 1    A + ▼ + A
            → Press ←

Row 2    + ✶ +
            ← Press →

Row 1    A + ▲ + A
            → Press ←

7. Butt, pin and sew rows together. Press Row 2 towards Row 1.

# SAILBOAT

Block Size: 8" (20.3cm) square finished
Seam allowance: 1/4" (5mm)

Shapes Used In This Pattern and How To Cut Them:

Shape A,B,C,F - Half Square Triangle - Page 17

Shape D - Rectangle - Page 18

Shape E - Full Trapezoid - Page 33

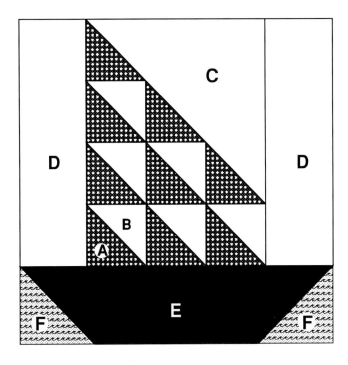

## CUTTING PROCEDURE:

A - Cut 1 - 2 3/8" x 13" (5.6 x 33cm) strip, medium dark. Cut into five 2 3/8" (5.6cm) squares. Recut in half diagonally. You will use only nine of these triangles.

B - Cut 3 - 2 3/8" (5.6cm) squares, light. Cut in half diagonally.

C - Cut 1 - 5 1/4" (12.9cm) square, light. Cut in half diagonally. You will only use one of the triangles.

D - Cut 2 - 2 1/4" x 6 1/2" (5.4 x 16.2cm) rectangles, light.

E - Cut 1 - 2 1/2" x 9 1/4" (6.1 x 22.8cm) rectangle, dark. Cut into a full trapezoid.

F - Cut 1 - 2 7/8" (6.8cm) square, medium light. Cut in half diagonally.

## SEWING PROCEDURE:

1. Sew A to B. Press to A. Make six sets.

2. Following the diagram, sew and press the AB squares and A triangles into rows. Cut dog ears off.

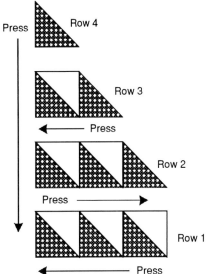

3. Sew C to the AB unit. Press to C. Cut dog ears off.

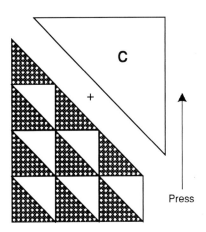

4. Sew D to each side of the ABC unit. Press to D.

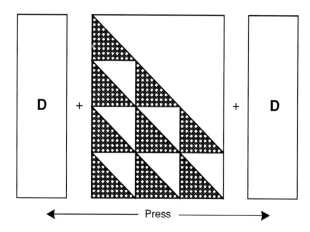

← Press →

5. Sew F to each side of E. Press to F. Cut dog ears off.

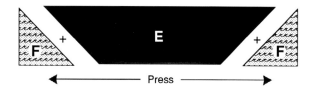

← Press →

6. Sew the EF unit to the bottom of the ABCD unit. Press to the EF unit.

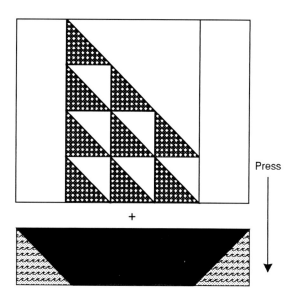

Press

*The background fabric was hand marblized by Peggy Schafer.*

# SCHOOL HOUSE

Block Size: 8" (20.3cm) square finished
Seam allowance: 1/4" (5mm)

Shapes Used In This Pattern and How To Cut Them:

Shape A,B,C,D,E,F,J - Rectangle - Page 18

Shape G,H - Half Square Triangle - Page 17

Shape I - Parallelogram - Page 22

Shape K - Square - Page 16

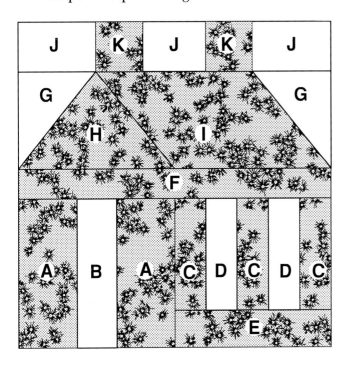

## CUTTING PROCEDURE FOR DARK FABRIC:

A - Cut 2 - 2" x 4 1/2" (4.8 x 11.2cm) rectangles, dark.

C - Cut 3 - 1 5/16" x 3 1/2" (3.3 x 8.6cm) rectangles, dark. (1 5/16" is between 1 1/4" and 1 3/8").

E - Cut 1 - 1 1/2" x 4 1/2" (3.5 x 11.2cm) rectangle, dark.

F - Cut 1 - 1 5/8" x 8 1/2" (3.9 x 21.3cm) rectangle, dark.

H - Cut 1 - 3 3/4" (9.1cm) square, dark. Cut in half diagonally. You will use only one of the triangles.

I - Cut 1 - 2 1/2" x 7 1/2" (6.1 x 18.6cm) rectangle, dark. Recut into one 3 3/8" (8.2cm) parallelogram. Left hand quilters cut with the wrong side of the fabric facing you. Right hand quilters cut with the right side of the fabric facing you.

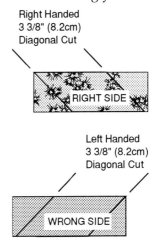

K - Cut 2 - 1 1/2" (3.5cm) squares, dark.

## CUTTING PROCEDURE FOR LIGHT FABRIC:

B - Cut 1 - 1 5/8" x 4 1/2" (3.8 x 11.2cm) rectangle, light.

D - Cut 2 - 1 5/16" x 3 1/2" (3.1 x 8.6cm) rectangles, light. (1 5/16" is located between 1 1/4" and 1 3/8").

G - Cut 1 - 2 7/8" (6.8cm) square, light. Cut in half diagonally.

J - Cut 3 - 1 1/2" x 2 1/2" (3.5 x 6.1cm) rectangles, light.

## SEWING PROCEDURE:

1. Door Section: Sew an A to each side of B. Press to A.

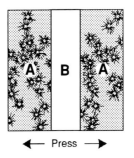

2. Window Section: Sew three Cs to the sides of two Ds. Press to C.

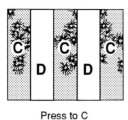

Press to C

3. Sew E to the bottom of the CD window section. Press to E.

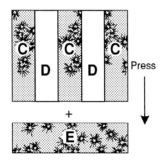

4. Sew the AB door section to the CDE window section. Press to the door section.

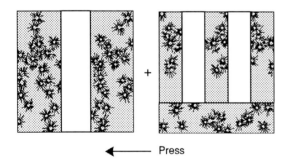

← Press

5. Sew F to the top of the door/window section. Press to F.

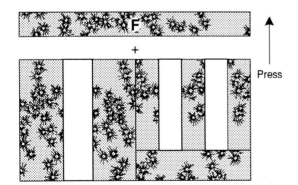

6. Roof Section - Sew H to I. (Offset these pieces by 1/4" (5mm) when sewing). Press to I.

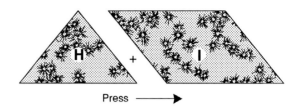

Press ⟶

7. Sew one G to each side of HI unit. Press to G.

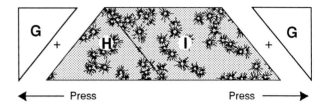

← Press          Press ⟶

8. Chimney Section - Sew according to the diagram. Press all seams towards K.

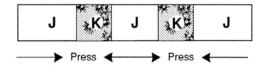

⟶ Press ←    ⟶ Press ←

9. Sew the roof section to the door/window section. Press to the door/window section. Sew the chimney section to the roof section. Press to the chimney section.

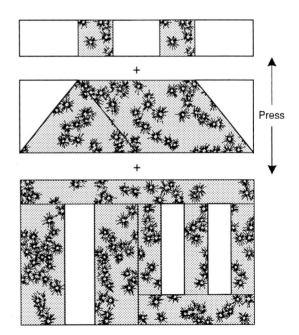

*School House Quilt made by the author for her son, Mark. Quilted by Joyce Isaacs.*

# SQUARE AND STAR

Block Size: 8" (20.3cm) square finished
Seam allowance: 1/4" (5mm)

Shapes Used In This Pattern and How To Cut Them:

    Shape A - Quarter Square Triangle - Page 18

    Shape B,D,E - Square - Page 16

    Shape C - Half Square Triangle - Page 17

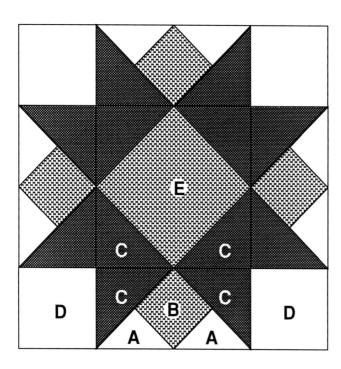

## CUTTING PROCEDURE:

A - Cut 2 - 3 1/4" (7.6cm) squares, light. Cut in half diagonally twice.

B - Cut 4 - 1 15/16" (4.7cm) squares, medium dark. (1 15/16" is located between 1 7/8" and 2").

C - Cut 6 - 2 7/8" (6.8cm) squares, dark. Cut in half diagonally.

D - Cut 4 - 2 1/2" (6.1cm) squares, light.

E - Cut 1 - 3 5/16" (8.1cm) square, medium dark. (3 5/16" is located between 3 1/4" and 3 3/8").

## SEWING PROCEDURE:

1. Sew A to the correct side of B. Press to A. Cut off the dog ears. Make four sets.

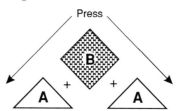

2. Sew C to each side of the AB set. Press to C. Cut off the dog ears. Make four units.

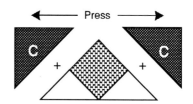

3. Sew two Cs to the opposite sides of E. Press to E. (C will appear too big, but it is not). Sew the two remaining Cs to the E square. Press to E. By pressing to E, you will be able to butt this unit with the ABC unit.

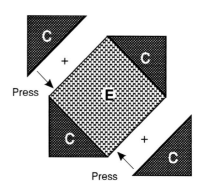

4. Butt, pin and sew into rows. Press according to the diagram.

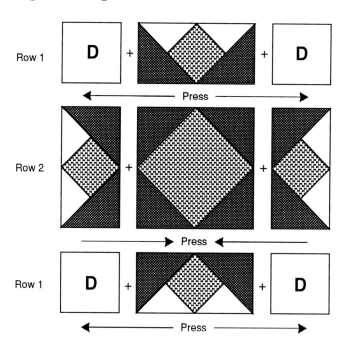

5. Butt, pin and sew rows together. Press Row 1 towards Row 2.

*NOTE: I cut a plastic template the same size as B and E. I placed the template on the flower motifs, drew around them and then rotary cut.*

# THOUSAND PYRAMID

Block Size: 8" (20.3cm) square finished
Seam allowance: 1/4" (5mm)

Shape Used In This Pattern and How To Cut It:

Shape A,B,C,D - Equilateral Triangle - Page 30

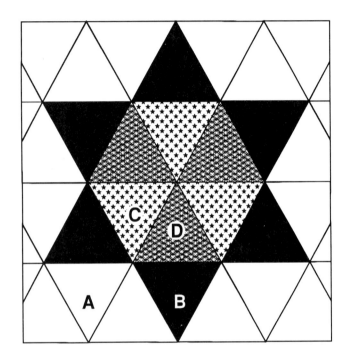

## CUTTING PROCEDURE:

A - Cut 1 - 2 3/4" x 44" (6.6 x 112cm) strip,
light. Cut into twenty four 60° equilateral
triangles.

B - Cut 1 - 2 3/4" x 13" (6.6 x 33cm) strip, dark.
Cut into six 60° equilateral triangles.

C - Cut 1 - 2 3/4" x 8" (6.6 x 20cm) strip,
medium light. Cut into three 60° equilateral triangles.

D - Cut 1 - 2 3/4" x 8" (6.6 x 20cm) strip,
medium dark. Cut into three 60° equilateral triangles.

## SEWING PROCEDURE:

1. Follow the diagram to sew and press into
rows. (Press after each equilateral triangle is sewn
on). Trim all dog ears before sewing rows together.

*NOTE: Be careful not to stretch the rows when sewing together.*

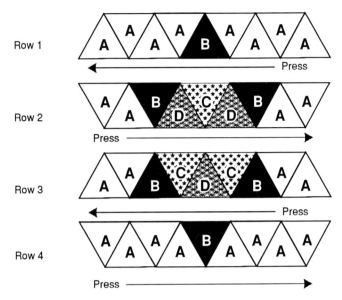

By pressing the seams in the direction shown, you
will be able to butt all the seams when sewing the
four rows together.

2. Sewing Rows Together - With the wrong
side of Row 1 facing you, sew to Row 2.

With the wrong side of Row 3 facing you, sew
to Row 2.

With the wrong side of Row 4 facing you, sew
to Row 3.

3. After sewing rows together, square up the
block to measure 8 1/2" (21.3cm) square, unfinished.

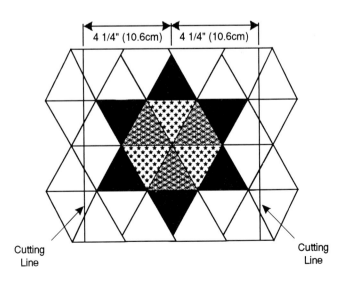

## GENERAL INFORMATION ON SEWING 60° EQUILATERAL TRIANGLES

This is the method I use for making my Thousand Pyramid Quilts and Miniatures. There are dozens of ways to arrange the colors in this pattern. Included is an uncolored diagram for your convenience. Let your creativity go!

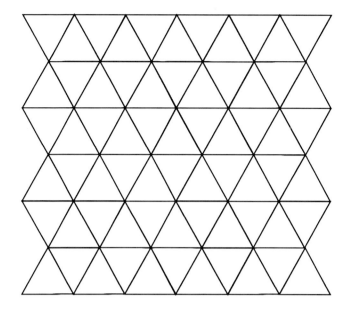

# TULIP BASKET

Block Size: 8" (20.3cm) square finished
Seam Allowance: 1/4" (5mm)

Shapes Used In This Pattern and How To Cut Them:

Shape A,B,C - 45° Diamond - Page 21

Shape D,H,I - Half Square Triangle - Page 17

Shape E - Quarter Square Triangle - Page 18

Shape F - Square - Page 16

Shape G - Rectangle - Page 18

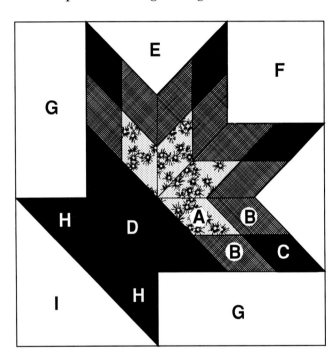

## CUTTING PROCEDURE:

A - Cut 1 - 1 3/8" x 12" (3.2 x 30.5cm) strip, medium light.

B - Cut 2 - 1 3/8" x 12" (3.2 x 30.5cm) strips, medium dark.

C - Cut 1 - 1 3/8" x 12" (3.2 x 30.5cm) strip, dark.

D - Cut 1 - 4 3/4" (10.6cm) square, dark. Cut in half diagonally. You will use only one of these triangles.

E - Cut 1 - 4 3/4" (11.4cm) square, light. Cut in half diagonally twice. You will use only two of the triangles.

F - Cut 1 - 3" (7.4cm) square, light.

G - Cut 2 - 2 1/2" x 4 1/2" (6.1 x 11.2cm) rectangles, light.

H - Cut 1 - 2 7/8" (6.8cm) square, dark. Cut in half diagonally.

I - Cut 1 - 4 7/8" (11.9cm) square, light. Cut in half diagonally. You will use only one of the triangles.

## SEWING PROCEDURE:

1. Pin the strips together according to the diagram. The strips are staggered 1" (2.5cm) in to allow for maximum use of fabric. Slowly sew SET 1 together. Press to A. Repeat for SET 2. Press SET 2 towards B.

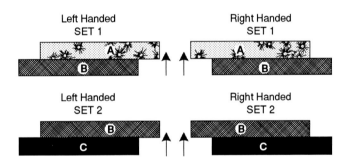

2. SET 1 - Using the 45° angle on the ruler as a guide, cut four 1 3/8" (3.2cm) diagonal strips. Repeat for SET 2.

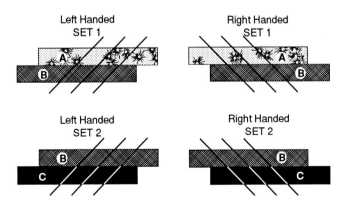

When you are cutting the 1 3/8" (3.2cm) strips make sure the 45° marking runs along the bottom of the strip and the ruler is 1 3/8" (3.2cm) in from the cut edge.

3. With the wrong side of the AB strip facing you; match, pin and sew the recut diagonal strips together to form four large diamonds. Press in the direction of the arrow. Cut off dog ears.

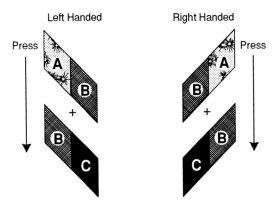

By pressing the seams in the direction shown, you will be able to butt all the seams when sewing the four large diamonds together.

4. Sewing the diamonds into pairs - Take two of the diamonds and pin together. Start sewing and stop 1/4" (5mm) from the bottom edge and back tack. Press according to the diagram. Cut off dog ears. Make two sets.

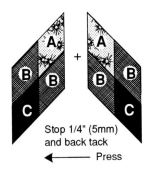

5. Sew two sets together to make a half. Remember to stop 1/4" (5mm) from the bottom edge and back tack. Press according to the diagram.

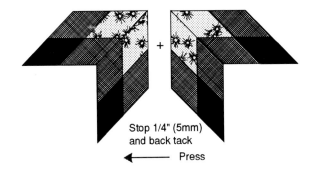

6. Sewing the E triangle to the tulip - With the wrong side of the diamond facing you, pin to the correct side of the E triangle. Start sewing from the outside tip of the diamond. Stop sewing when you reach the other seam and back tack.

Cut the thread and remove from the machine. Now with the wrong side of the E triangle facing you, pin and sew to the diamond. Stop sewing when you reach the other seam and back tack. Press to E. Repeat for the other side. Cut off all dog ears.

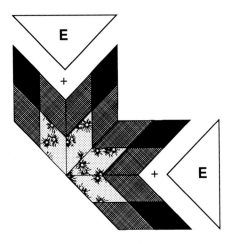

7. Sewing the F square to the tulip - With the wrong side of the tulip facing you, pin to one side of the F square. Start sewing. Stop sewing when you reach the other seam and back tack. Cut the thread and remove from the machine.

Now with the wrong side of F facing you, pin to the other diamond. Start sewing. Stop sewing when you reach the other seam and back tack. Press to F.

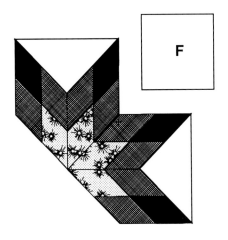

8. Sew D triangle to the top unit. Press to D.

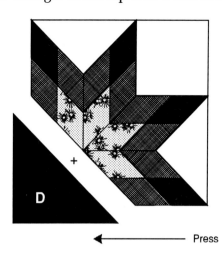

Press ←——————

9. Sew H triangle to G. Press to G. H triangle tip will hang over slightly. Do not trim. (You will use these tips when adding on I).

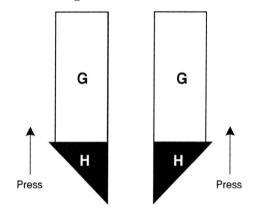

Press ↑      ↑ Press

10. Sew the GH unit to the proper sides. Press to GH.

←—— Press

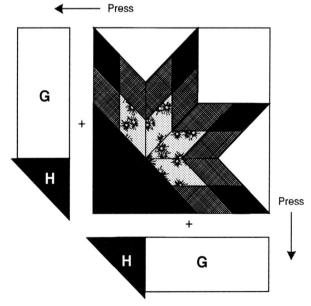

Press ↓

11. Sew I to the basket. Note: H triangle tips will line up with the two tips of I triangle. Press to I.

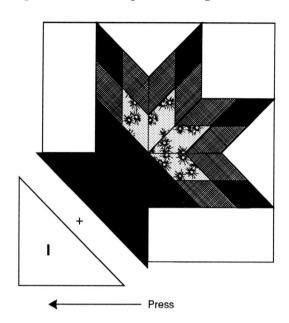

←——————— Press

*Tulip Basket*

*Uncle Lee's Puzzle*

# UNCLE LEE'S PUZZLE

Block Size: 8" (20.3cm) square finished
Seam allowance: 1/4" (5mm)

Shapes Used In This Pattern and How To Cut Them:

Shape A, B, D, F - Half Square Triangle - Page 17

Shape C - Quarter Square Triangle - Page 18

Shape E - Full Trapezoid - Page 33

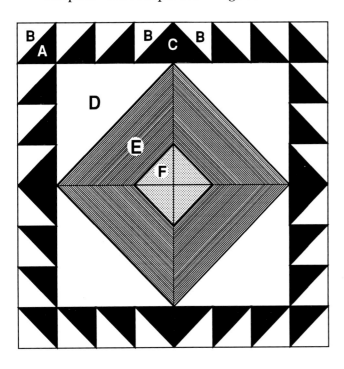

## CUTTING PROCEDURE:

A - Cut 1 - 1 7/8" x 20" (4.3 x 51cm) strip, dark.

B - Cut 1 - 1 7/8" x 28" (4.3 x 71cm) strip, light.

Position the light strip on top of the dark strip, right sides together. Cut into ten 1 7/8" (4.3cm) squares. Recut the squares in half diagonally.

Cut the remaining light strip into four 1 7/8" (4.3cm) squares. Recut the squares in half diagonally. (You will use these with the C piece).

C - Cut 1 - 3 1/4" (7.6cm) square, dark. Cut in half diagonally twice.

D - Cut 2 - 3 7/8" (9.4cm) squares, light. Cut in half diagonally.

E - Cut 4 - 1 7/8" x 5 1/2" (4.5 x 13.3cm) rectangles, medium. Cut into four full trapezoids.

F - Cut 2 - 1 7/8" (4.3cm) squares, medium light. Cut in half diagonally.

## SEWING PROCEDURE:

1. Sew A to B. Press to A. Make twenty squares.

Press →

2. Sew one B to the side of C. Press to B. Sew another B to the other side of C. Press to B. Cut off dog ears. Make four sets.

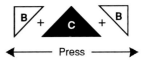

← Press →

3. Sew two AB squares to each side of the BC piece. See diagram. Press away from the BC piece. Make two rows like this.

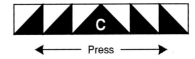

← Press →

4. Sew three AB squares to each side of the BC piece. See diagram. Press away from the BC piece. Make two rows like this.

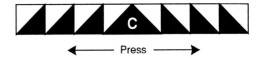

← Press →

5. Sew D to E. Add F. Make four sets. Press D and F **towards** E on two of the sets and press D and F **away** from E on the other two sets.

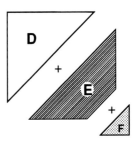

6. Butt, pin and sew two of the DEF sets together. (Make sure one of the sets is pressed towards E and one pressed away from E). Make two rows.

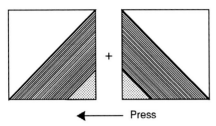

← Press

7. Butt, pin and sew the two rows together. It doesn't matter which way you press this seam.

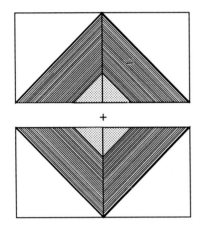

8. Sew a short ABC row to each side of the center square. Press towards the center square.

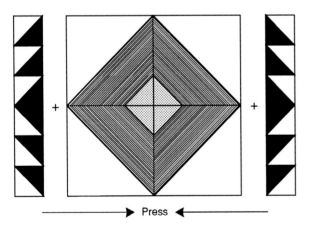

Press

9. Sew a long ABC row to the top and bottom. Press towards the center square.

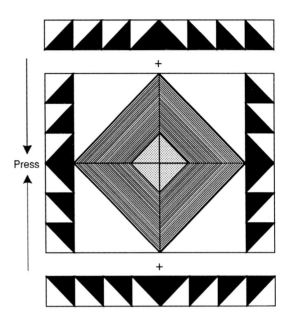

Press

# WILD GOOSE CHASE

Block Size: 8" (20.3cm) square finished
Seam allowance: 1/4" (5mm)

Shapes Used In This Pattern and How To Cut Them:

Shape A - Quarter Square Triangle - Page 18

Shape B - Half Square Triangle - Page 17

Shape C,D - Square - Page 16

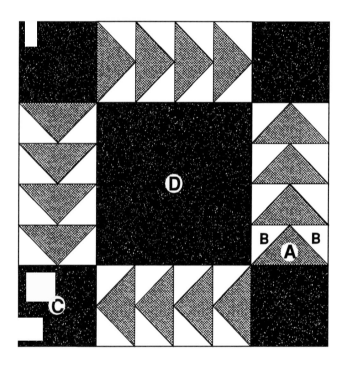

## CUTTING PROCEDURE:

A - Cut 4 - 3 1/4" (7.6cm) squares, medium dark. Cut in half diagonally twice.

B - Cut 1 - 2" x 34" (4.6 x 86.4cm) strip, light. Cut into sixteen 2" (4.6cm) squares. Recut in half diagonally. (These pieces are slightly oversized).

C - Cut 4 - 2 1/2" (6.1cm) squares, dark.

D - Cut 1 - 4 1/2" (11.2cm) square, dark.

## SEWING PROCEDURE:

1. Sew one B to A. Press to B. Add another B to the other side of A. Press to B. Cut off dog ears. Make sixteen sets.

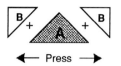

2. If necessary, trim B to within 1/4" (5mm) of the top of the goose. Each goose will measure 1 1/2" x 2 1/2" (3.5 x 6.1cm).

3. To form a row, sew four geese together. Press according to the diagram. Make four sets.

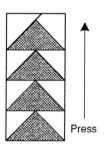

4. Butt, pin and sew into rows. Press according to the diagram.

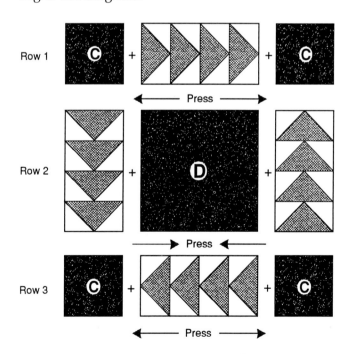

5. Butt, pin and sew rows together. Press Row 1 and Row 3 towards Row 2.

# BACHELOR'S PUZZLE

Block Size: 10" (25.4cm) square finished
Seam allowance: 1/4" (5mm)

Shapes Used In This Pattern and How To Cut Them:

Shape A,B - Prism - Page 39

Shape C - Quarter Square Triangle - Page 18

Shape D,F - Square - Page 16

Shape E - Rectangle - Page 18

Shape G - Half Square Triangle - Page 17

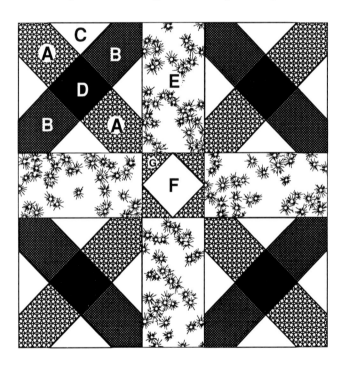

## CUTTING PROCEDURE:

A - Cut 8 - 1 3/4" x 2 3/4" (4.2 x 6.6cm) rectangles, medium dark. Cut each into a prism shape.

B - Cut 8 - 1 3/4" x 2 3/4" (4.2 x 6.6cm) rectangles, contrasting medium dark. Cut each into a prism shape.

C - Cut 4 - 3 3/8" (7.9cm) squares, light. Cut in half diagonally twice.

D - Cut 4 - 1 3/4" (4.2cm) squares, dark.

E - Cut 4 - 2 3/4" x 4 3/8" (6.7 x 10.8cm) rectangles, medium light.

F - Cut 1 - 2 1/8" (5.1cm) square, light.

G - Cut 2 - 2" (4.6cm) squares, medium dark. Cut in half diagonally.

## SEWING PROCEDURE:

1. Sew one C to each side of B. Press to B. Make eight sets. This is the side section.

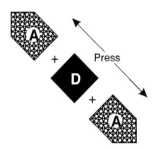

2. Sew one A to the top and bottom of D. Press to A. Make four sets. This is the middle section.

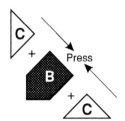

3. Sew a side section (BC) to the middle section (AD). Press to the middle section. Add another side section to the other side. Press to the middle section. Make four sets.

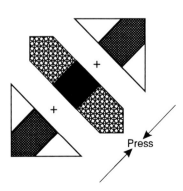

4. Sew two Gs to the opposite sides of F. Press to G. Add G to the other two sides. Press to G.

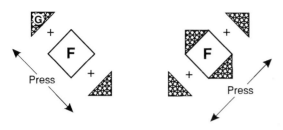

5. Pin and sew into rows. Press according to the diagram.

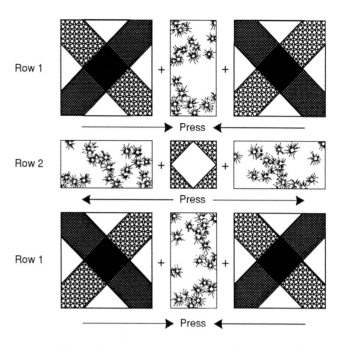

Row 1

Press

Row 2

Press

Row 1

Press

6. Butt, pin and sew rows together. Press Row 2 towards Row 1.

# FLYING GEESE

Block Size: 10" (25.4cm) square finished
Seam allowance: 1/4" (5mm)

Shapes Used In This Pattern and How To Cut Them:

Shape A,C - Quarter Square Triangle - Page 18

Shape B,D - Half Square Triangle - Page 17

Shape E - Square - Page 16

## CUTTING PROCEDURE:

A - Cut 3 - 4 1/16" (9.6cm) squares, light. (4 1/16" is located between 4" and 4 1/8"). Cut in half diagonally twice.

B - Cut 12 - 2 5/16" (5.4cm) squares, dark. (2 5/16" is located between 2 1/4" and 2 3/8"). Cut in half diagonally.

C - Cut 1 - 7 1/4" (17.7cm) square, medium light. Cut in half diagonally twice.

D - Cut 2 - 3" (7.1cm) squares, dark. Cut in half diagonally.

E - Cut 1 - 3 5/16" (8.1cm) square, dark. (3 5/16" is located between 3 1/4" and 3 3/8").

## SEWING PROCEDURE:

1. Sew one B to the side of A. Press to B. Add another B to the other side of A. Press to B. Make twelve geese.

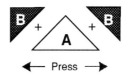

2. Sew three geese together to form a row. Make four rows.

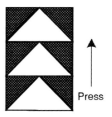

3. Sew one C to each side of a row of geese. Press to C. Make two sets. These are the sides of the block.

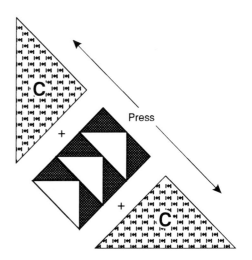

4. Sew E to two rows of geese. Press to E. This is the center of the block.

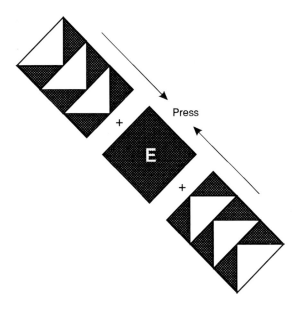

Press

5. Sew the side sections (ABC) to the center section (ABE). Press to the side sections (ABC). Sew one D to each corner. Press towards D. "Square Up" D if necessary.

# FOLLOW THE LEADER

Block Size: 10" (25.4cm) square finished
Seam allowance: 1/4" (5mm)

Shapes Used In This Pattern and How To Cut Them:

Shape A,H - Square - Page 16

Shape B,C - Half Square Triangle - Page 17

Shape D,E - Quarter Square Triangle - Page 18

Shape F,G - Half Rectangle - Page 20

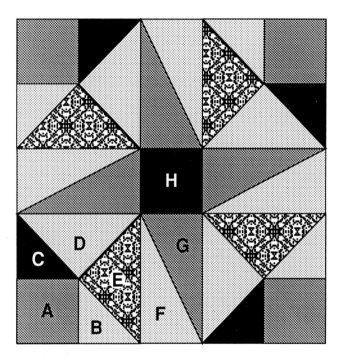

## CUTTING PROCEDURE:

A - Cut 4 - 2 1/2" (6.1cm) squares, medium dark.

B - Cut 2 - 2 7/8" (6.8cm) squares, light. Cut in half diagonally.

C - Cut 2 - 2 7/8" (6.8cm) squares, dark. Cut in half diagonally.

D - Cut 1 - 5 1/4" (12.7cm) square, light. Cut in half diagonally twice.

E - Cut 1 - 5 1/4" (12.7cm) square, medium light. Cut in half diagonally twice.

F - Cut 2 - 2 11/16" x 5 3/8" (6.5 x 13.1cm) rectangles, light. (2 11/16" is located between 2 5/8" and 2 3/4"). With the right side facing you, cut in half diagonally, as shown.

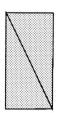

G - Cut 2 - 2 11/16" x 5 3/8" (6.5 x 13.1cm) rectangles, dark. (2 11/16" is located between 2 5/8" and 2 3/4") With the right side facing you, cut in half diagonally, as shown.

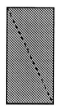

H - Cut 1 - 2 1/2" (6.1cm) square, dark.

## SEWING PROCEDURE:

1. Sew A to B. Press to B. Add C to the other side of A. Press to C. Make four sets.

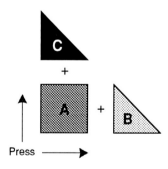

2. Sew D to E. Press to D. Make four sets.

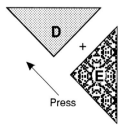

112

3. Sew one ABC set to a DE set. Press to DE. Make four units.

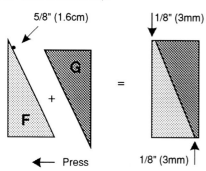

Press

4. Sew F to G. When sewing F to G, offset the two pieces by 5/8" (1.6cm). Measure 5/8" (1.6cm) on the diagonal edge of F and place a pencil mark there. Place the bottom of G there and start sewing. Press to F. Trim dog ears. There will be a 1/8" (3mm) offset of the pieces in the corner. See diagram. The sewn rectangle will measure 2 1/2" x 4 1/2" (6.1 x 11.2cm).

5/8" (1.6cm)   1/8" (3mm)

G

F   +   =

◄— Press   1/8" (3mm)

5. Butt, pin and sew into rows. Press according to the diagram.

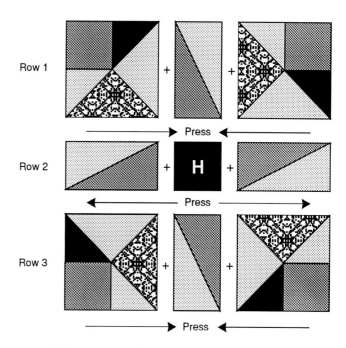

Row 1   +   +

——► Press ◄——

Row 2   +   H   +

◄—— Press ——►

Row 3   +   +

——► Press ◄——

6. Butt, pin and sew rows together. Press Row 1 towards Row 2.

# GARDEN OF EDEN

Block Size: 10" (25.4cm) square finished
Seam allowance: 1/4" (5mm)

Shapes Used In This Pattern and How To Cut Them:

    Shape A,D,E - Square - Page 16

    Shape B, C Half Square Triangle - Page 17

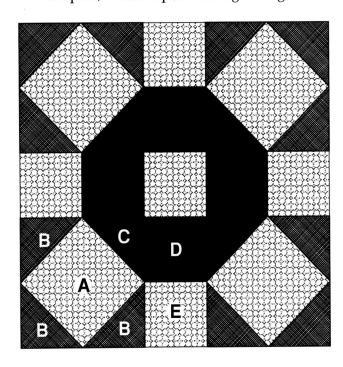

## CUTTING PROCEDURE:

A - Cut 4 - 3 3/8" (8.3cm) squares, light.

B - Cut 6 - 2 7/8" (6.8cm) squares, medium light. Cut in half diagonally.

C - Cut 2 - 2 7/8" (6.8cm) squares, dark. Cut in half diagonally.

D - Cut 4 - 2 1/2" (6.1cm) squares, dark.

E - Cut 5 - 2 1/2" (6.1cm) squares, light.

## SEWING PROCEDURES:

1. Sew B to the opposite sides of A. Press to B. Make four sets.

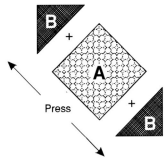

2. Sew B and C to the remaining two sides of A. Press to B and C. Make four sets.

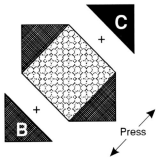

3. Sew D to E. Press to E. Make four sets.

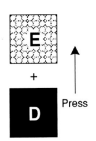

4. Sew the remaining E to two of the DE sets. Press to the D pieces.

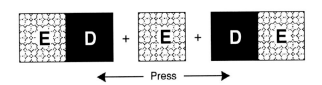

5. Pin and sew into rows according to the diagram.

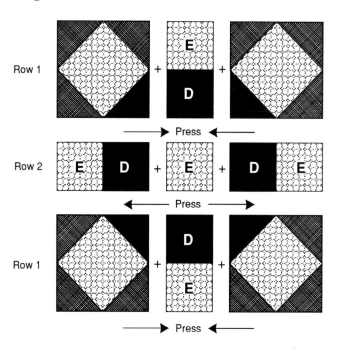

6. Butt, pin and sew rows together. Press Row 1 towards Row 2.

# GOING HOME

Block Size: 10" (25.4cm) square finished
Seam allowance: 1/4" (5mm)

Shapes Used In This Pattern and How To Cut Them:

Shape A,B - Half Square Triangle - Page 17

Shape C,D - Quarter Square Triangle - Page 18

Shape E - Prism - Page 39

Shape F,G - Square - Page 16

## Cutting Procedure:

A - Cut 6 - 2 5/16" (5.4cm) squares, medium light. (2 5/16" is located between 2 1/4" and 2 3/8"). Cut in half diagonally.

B - Cut 2 - 2 5/16" (5.4cm) squares, dark. (2 5/16" is located between 2 1/4" and 2 3/8"). Cut in half diagonally.

C - Cut 1 - 5 1/4" (12.7cm) square, medium dark. Cut in half diagonally twice.

D - Cut 2 - 5 1/4" (12.7cm) squares, light. Cut in half diagonally twice.

E - Cut 4 - 2" x 5 1/2" (4.8 x 13.6cm) rectangles, contrasting medium dark. Cut each into a prism shape.

F - Cut 4 - 2" (4.8cm) squares, dark.

G - Cut 1 - 2" (4.8cm) square, medium light.

## Sewing Procedure:

1. Sew A to B. Press to B. Make four sets.

2. Sew one A to the correct side of the AB square. Press to A. Add another A to the other side of the AB square. Press to A. Make four sets.

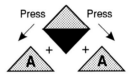

3. Sew C to the AB set. Press to C. Make four sets.

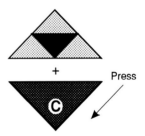

4. Sew D to one side of the ABC square. Press to D. Sew another D to the other side of the ABC square. Press to D. Make four sets.

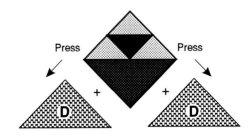

5. Sew E to F. Press to F. Make four sets.

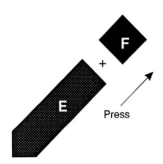

6. Sew G to two of the EF sets. Press to EF.

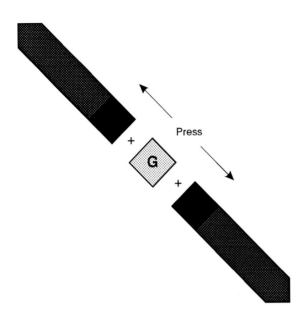

7. Sew an ABCD unit to each side of the remaining EF sections. Press to EF. Make two sets.

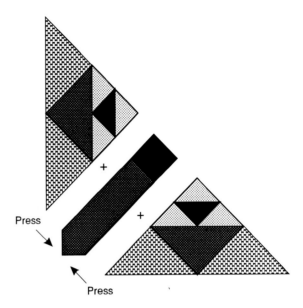

8. Butt, pin and sew the rows together according to the diagram. Press to the EFG section.

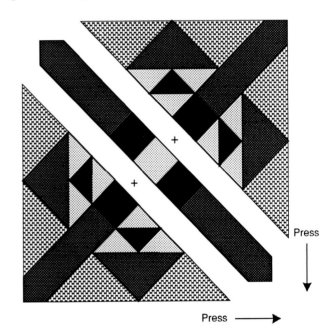

*Going Home*

*Jack In The Box*

# JACK IN THE BOX

Block Size: 10" (25.4cm) square finished
Seam allowance: 1/4" (5mm)

Shapes Used In This Pattern and How To Cut Them:

Shape A - Half Square Triangle - Page 17

Shape B - Quarter Square Triangle - Page 18

Shape C - Parallelogram - Page 22

Shape D - Rectangle - Page 18

Shape E - Square - Page 16

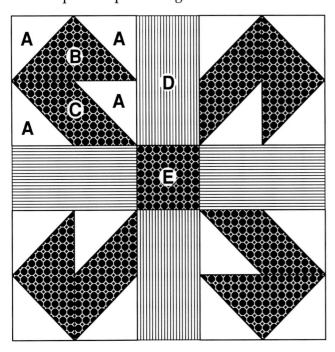

## CUTTING PROCEDURE

A - Cut 8 - 2 7/8" (6.8cm) squares, light. Cut in half diagonally.

B - Cut 1 - 5 1/4" (12.7cm) square, dark. Cut in half diagonally twice.

C - Cut 1 - 2 1/2" x 17" (6.1 x 43cm) strip, dark. Left hand quilters cut with the wrong side of the fabric facing you. Right hand quilters cut with the right side of the fabric facing you. Make four 1 7/8" (4.6cm) diagonal cuts.

D - Cut 4 - 2 1/2" x 4 1/2" (6.1 x 11.2cm) rectangles, medium.

E - Cut 1 - 2 1/2" (6.1cm) square, dark.

## SEWING PROCEDURE:

1. Sew one A to B. Press to A. Sew another A to the other side of B. Press to A. Make four sets.

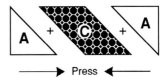

2. Sew one A to each side of C. Press to C. Make four sets.

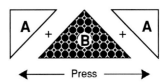

3. Butt, pin and sew the AB set to the AC set. Press to the AC set.

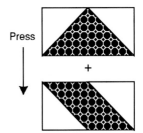

4. Pin and sew into rows. Press according to the diagram.

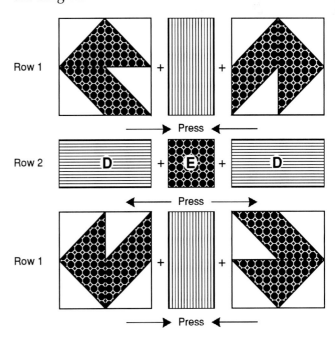

5. Butt, pin and sew rows together. Press Row 1 towards Row 2.

# KAREN'S STAR

Block Size: 10" (25.4cm) square finished
Seam allowance: 1/4" (5mm)

Shapes Used In This Pattern and How To Cut Them:

Shape A,F - Square - Page 16

Shape B,C - Half Square Triangle - Page 17

Shape D - Half Rectangle - Page 20

Shape E - Odd Shaped Triangle - See letter E for cutting

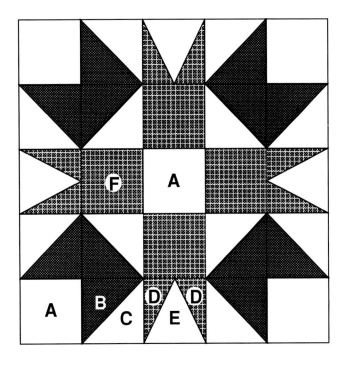

## CUTTING PROCEDURE:

A - Cut 5 - 2 1/2" (6.1cm) squares, light.

B - Cut 6 - 2 7/8" (6.8cm) squares, dark. Cut in half diagonally.

C - Cut 6 - 2 7/8" (6.8cm) squares, light. Cut in half diagonally.

D - Cut 4 - 1 11/16" x 3 1/4" (3.9 x 7.7cm) rectangles, medium dark. (1 11/16" is between 1 5/8" and 1 3/4"). With right side of fabric facing you, cut two of the

rectangles left to right and the other two rectangles right to left to create mirror images. See the diagram.

Left to Right          Right to Left

E - Cut 4 - 2 3/4" x 2 7/8" (6.6 x 6.8cm) rectangles. Fold the rectangle in half and put a pencil mark along the top of the fold line. With the ruler and cutter, cut from the bottom corner to the pencil mark. See diagram.

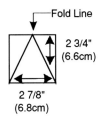

Fold Line

2 3/4" (6.6cm)

2 7/8" (6.8cm)

F - Cut 4 - 2 1/2" (6.1cm) squares, medium dark.

## SEWING PROCEDURE:

1. Sew B to C. Make twelve squares. Press eight to the dark and four to the light. I have marked on the diagram in #3 where you will use the squares pressed to the light. The reason for this is so you can butt the seams together.

2. Match the top of one D to the top of E. Sew on the diagonal. Press to D. Add another D to the other side. Press to D. Cut off the dog ears. When D and E are stitched together, the seam will be offset from the corner 1/8" (3mm). This section will measure 2 1/2" (6.1cm) square. Make four sets.

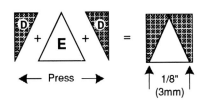

← Press →          1/8" (3mm)

3. Butt, pin and sew into rows. Press according to the diagram.

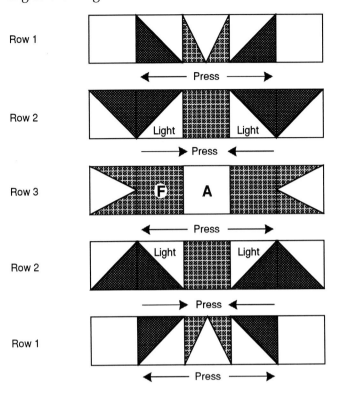

Row 1

Press

Row 2

Light                    Light

Press

Row 3

F        A

Press

Row 2

Light        Light

Press

Row 1

Press

4. Butt, pin and sew rows together. Press Rows 1 and 2 towards Row 3.

# KING DAVID'S CROWN

Block Size: 10" (25.4cm) square finished
Seam allowance: 1/4" (5mm)

Shapes Used In This Pattern and How To Cut Them:

Shape A,I - Square  - Page 16

Shape B,C,G - Half Square Triangle  - Page 17

Shape D,E,F - Quarter Square Triangle - Page 18

Shape H - Full Trapezoid - Page 33

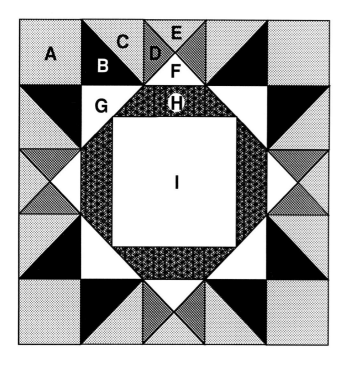

## CUTTING PROCEDURE:

A -  Cut 4 - 2 1/2" (6.1cm) squares, medium light.

B -  Cut 4 - 2 7/8" (6.8cm) squares, dark. Cut in half diagonally.

C -  Cut 4 -  2 7/8" (6.8cm) squares, medium light. Cut in half diagonally.

D -  Cut 2 - 3 1/4" (7.6cm) squares, medium dark.  Cut in half diagonally twice.

E -  Cut 1 - 3 1/4" (7.6cm) square, medium light.  Cut in half diagonally twice.

F -  Cut 1 - 3 1/4" (7.6cm) square, light. Cut in half diagonally twice.

G -  Cut 2 - 2 7/8" (6.8cm) squares, light.  Cut in half diagonally.

H -  Cut 4 - 1 1/2" x 5 1/4" (3.5 x 12.7cm) rectangles, contrasting medium dark. Cut each  into a full trapezoid shape.

I - Cut 1 - 4 1/2" (11.2cm) square, light.

## SEWING PROCEDURE:

1. Sew B to C.  Press to B.  Make eight sets.

2. Sew E to D.  Press to D.  Make four sets.

3. Sew D to F.  Press to D.  Make four sets.

4. Sew the DE set to the DF set.  Press towards the DE set.  Make four units.

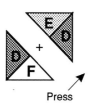

5. Sew H to the top and bottom of I. Press to H. Sew the remaining two H pieces to the sides of I. Press to H.

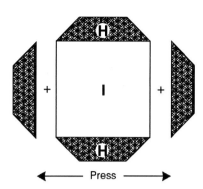

6. Sew G to the corners of the HI unit. Press to G.

7. To Make Row 1: Sew two BC squares to the DEF unit. Press to the DEF unit. Make four units.

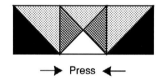

8. Add an A square to each end of two of the BC/DEF units. Press to A.

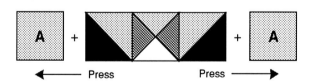

9. To Make Row 2: Sew one BC/DEF unit to each side of the HI piece. Press to the HI piece.

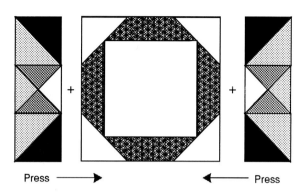

10. Butt, pin and sew rows together. Press Row 1 towards Row 2.

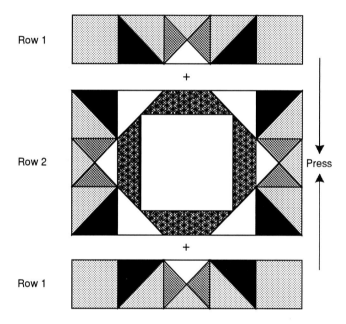

*King David's Crown*

*Michigan Beauty*

# MICHIGAN BEAUTY

Block Size: 10" (25.4cm) square finished
Seam allowance: 1/4" (5mm)

Shapes Used In This Pattern and How To Cut Them:

Shape A - Square - Page 16

Shape B - Quarter Square Triangle - Page 18

Shape C,CR,D,DR - Parallelogram - Page 22

Shape E - Half Square Triangle - Page 17

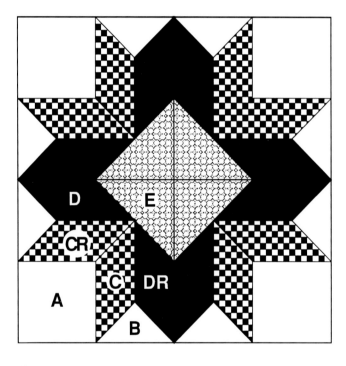

## CUTTING PROCEDURE:

A - Cut 4 - 3" (7.4cm) squares, light.

B - Cut 2 - 3 3/4" (8.9cm) squares, light. Cut in half diagonally twice.

C - Cut 1- 1 3/4" x 18" (4.2 x 46cm) strip, medium dark. Left hand quilters cut with the wrong side of the fabric facing you. Right hand quilters cut with the right side facing you. Make four 2 1/4" (5.6cm) diagonal cuts.

CR - Cut 1 - 1 3/4" x 18" (4.2 x 46cm) strip, medium dark. Left hand quilters cut with the right side of the fabric facing you. Right hand quilters cut with the wrong side facing you. Make four 2 1/4" (5.6cm) diagonal cuts.

D - Cut 1 - 1 3/4" x 18" (4.2 x 46cm) strip, dark. Left hand quilters cut with the wrong side of the fabric facing you. Right hand quilters cut with the right side facing you. Make four 2 1/4" (5.6cm) diagonal cuts.

DR - Cut 1 - 1 3/4" x 18" (4.2 x 46cm) strip, dark. Left hand quilters cut with the right side of the fabric facing you. Right hand quilters cut with the wrong side facing you. Make four 2 1/4" (5.6cm) diagonal cuts.

E - Cut 2 - 3 3/8" (8.1cm) squares, medium light. Cut in half diagonally.

## SEWING PROCEDURE:

1. Start sewing D to CR. Stop sewing 1/4" (5mm) from the bottom edge and back tack. Press to D. Cut dog ear off. Make four sets.

Stop sewing 1/4" (5mm)
and back tack
← Press

2. Start sewing C to DR. Stop sewing 1/4" (5mm) from the bottom edge and back tack. Press to C. Cut dog ear off. Make four sets.

Stop sewing 1/4" (5mm)
and back tack
← Press

3. Start sewing a D/CR set to a C/DR set. Stop sewing 1/4" (5mm) from the bottom edge and back tack. Press to the D/CR set. Make four units.

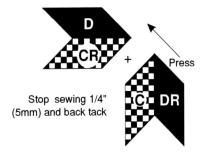

4. Sewing the B triangle to each set - With the wrong side of D facing you, pin to the correct side of the B triangle. Start sewing from the outside tip of the parallelogram. Stop sewing when you reach the other seam and back tack.

Cut the thread and remove from the machine. Now with the wrong side of the B triangle facing you, pin and sew to the parallelogram. Stop sewing when you reach the other seam and back tack. Press towards B. Repeat for the other side. Cut off dog ears. Do all four units this way.

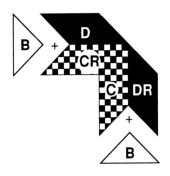

5. Sewing A square to the unit - With the wrong side of CR facing you, pin to the correct side of the A square. Start sewing. Stop sewing when you reach the other seam and back tack. Cut the thread and remove from the machine.

Now with the wrong side of A facing you, pin to C. Start sewing. Stop sewing when you reach the other seam and back tack. Press towards A. Do this to all four units.

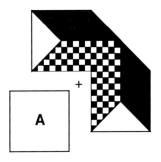

6. Sew E to the unit. Press to E. Do this to all four units.

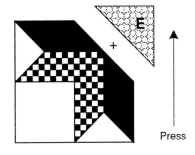

7. Carefully match, pin and sew into rows. Press according to the diagram.

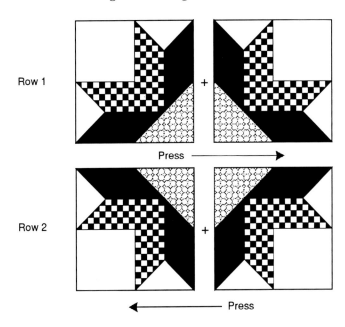

8. Carefully match, pin and sew rows together. Press Row 1 towards Row 2.

# RUBY'S FAVORITE

Block Size: 10" (25.4cm) square finished
Seam allowance: 1/4" (5mm)

Shapes Used In This Pattern and How To Cut Them:

    Shape A,B,D,I - Half Square Triangle - Page 17

    Shape C - Rectangle - Page 18

    Shape E - Full Trapezoid - Page 33

    Shape F,H - Square - Page 16

    Shape G - Quarter Square Triangle - Page 18

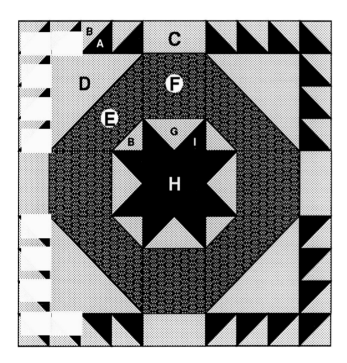

## CUTTING PROCEDURE:

A - Cut 1 - 1 7/8" x 28" (4.3 x 71.1cm) strip, dark.

B - Cut 1 - 1 7/8" x 32" (4.3 x 81.3cm) strip, light.

    Position the light strip on top of the dark strip, right sides together. Cut into fourteen 1 7/8" (4.3cm) squares. Recut the squares in half diagonally.

Cut the remaining light strip into two 1 7/8" (4.3cm) squares. Recut the squares in half diagonally. (You will be sewing these to the E piece).

C - Cut 4 - 1 1/2" x 2 1/2" (3.5 x 6.1cm) rectangles, light.

D - Cut 2 - 3 7/8" (9.4cm) squares, light. Cut in half diagonally.

E - Cut 4 - 1 7/8" x 5 1/2" (4.5 x 13.3cm) rectangles, medium dark. Cut into four full trapezoids.

F - Cut 4 - 2 1/2" (6.1cm) squares, medium dark.

G - Cut 1 - 3 1/4" (7.6cm) square, light. Cut in half diagonally twice.

H - Cut 1 - 2 1/2" (6.1cm) square, dark.

I - Cut 4 - 1 7/8" (4.3cm) squares, dark. Cut in half diagonally.

## SEWING PROCEDURE:

1. Sew A to B. Press to A. Make twenty eight sets.

Press →

2. Sew D to E. Add B. Press seams towards E piece. Make four units.

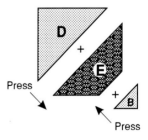

Press

Press

3. Sew one I to the side of G. Press to I. Sew another I to the other side of G. Press to I. Make four sets.

← Press →

4. Sew one GI unit to F. Press to F. Make four units.

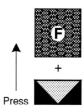

Press

5. Sew and press the AB squares into rows according to the diagram in step 6.

6. Pin and sew into rows. Press according to the diagram.

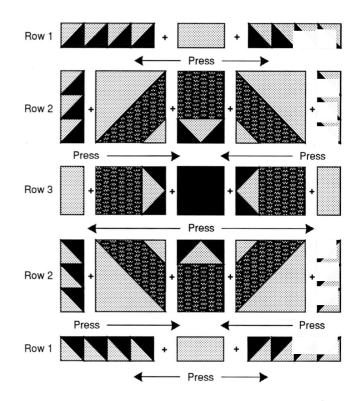

7. Butt, pin and sew rows together. Press Row 1 and 2 towards Row 3.

# S.O.S. PINWHEEL

(Save Our Scraps Pinwheel)

Block Size: 10" (25.4 cm) square finished
Seam allowance: 1/4" (5mm)

Shapes Used In This Pattern and How To Cut Them:

Shape A, A1 - Quarter Square Triangle - Page 18

Shape B, B1 - Kite Shape - Page 36

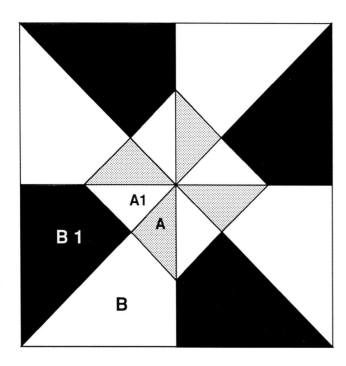

## CUTTING PROCEDURE:

A - Cut 1 - 4 3/8" (10.4cm) square, medium dark. Cut in half diagonally, twice.

A1 - Cut 1 - 4 3/8" (10.4cm) square, light. Cut square in half diagonally, twice.

B - Cut 2 - 6" (14.8cm) squares, light. Cut in half diagonally.

With the RIGHT side of the fabric facing you, cut into the kite shape. By cutting the

kite shape this way, you will NOT have the bias on the outside edges of the block.

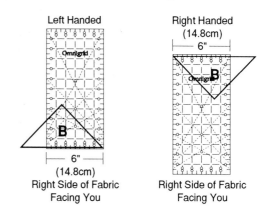

B1 - Cut 2 - 6" (14.8cm) squares, dark. Cut in half diagonally.

With the WRONG side of the fabric facing you, cut into the kite shape. By cutting the kite shape this way, you will NOT have the bias on the outside edges of the block.

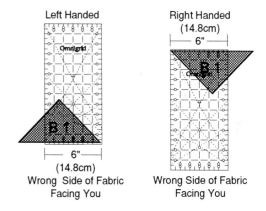

## SEWING PROCEDURE:

1. Sew one light A1 to a dark B1. Press to the dark.

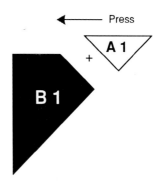

2. Sew one medium dark A to one light B. Press to the A.

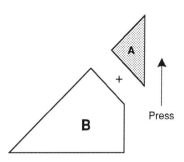

3. Butt, pin and sew the A1/B1 section to the AB section. Press to the A1/B1 section. Make four units.

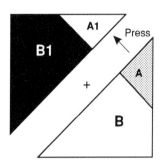

4. Butt, pin and sew into rows. Press according to the diagram.

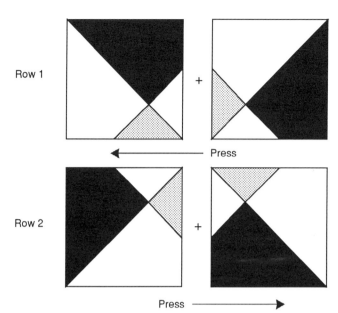

5. Butt, pin and sew the rows together. Press Row 1 towards Row 2.

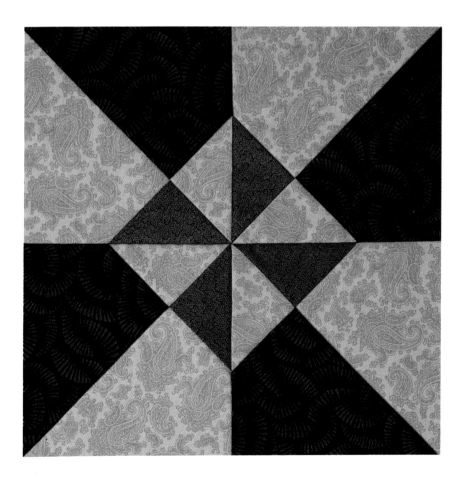

# SQUARE AND A HALF

Block Size: 10" (25.4cm) square finished
Seam allowance: 1/4" (5mm)

Shapes Used In This Pattern and How To Cut Them:

Shape A,B - Half Square Triangle - Page 17

Shape C - Full Trapezoid - Page 33

Shape D,E,F - Quarter Square Triangle - Page 18

Shape G - Square - Page 16

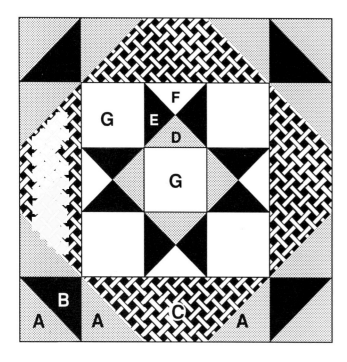

## CUTTING PROCEDURE:

A - Cut 6 - 2 7/8" (6.8cm) squares, medium light. Cut in half diagonally.

B - Cut 2 - 2 7/8" (6.8cm) squares, dark. Cut in half diagonally.

C - Cut 4 - 2 1/2" x 7 1/4" (6.1 x 17.7cm) rectangles, medium dark. Cut into four full trapezoids.

D - Cut 1 - 3 1/4" (7.6cm) square, medium light. Cut in half diagonally twice.

E - Cut 2 - 3 1/4" (7.6cm) squares, dark. Cut in half diagonally twice.

F - Cut 1 - 3 1/4" (7.6cm) square, light. Cut in half diagonally twice.

G - Cut 5 - 2 1/2" (6.1cm) squares, light.

## SEWING PROCEDURE:

1. Sew E to D. Press to E. Make four sets.

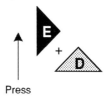

2. Sew E to F. Press to E. Make four sets.

3. Sew the ED set to the EF set. Press to the ED set.

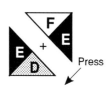

4. Pin and sew into rows. Press according to the diagram. Butt, pin and sew rows together. Press Row 2 towards Row 1.

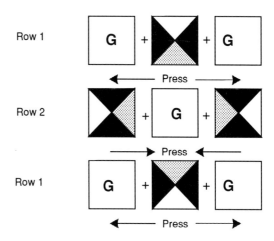

5. Sew A to B.  Press to B.  Make four sets.

Press ⟶

6. Sew one A to each side of C.  Press to A. Make four sets.

◄── Press ──►

7. Pin and sew into rows.  Press according to the diagram.

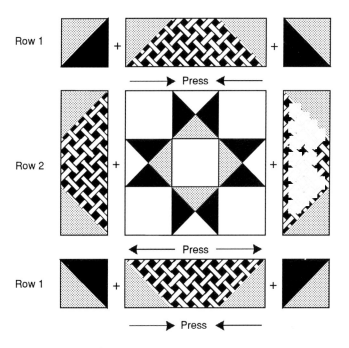

Row 1

──► Press ◄──

Row 2

◄── Press ──►

Row 1

──► Press ◄──

8. Butt, pin and sew rows together. Press Row 2 towards Row 1.

# BEGGAR'S BLOCK

Block Size: 12" (30.5cm) square finished
Seam allowance: 1/4" (5mm)

Shapes Used In This Pattern and How To Cut Them:

Shape A,D - Full Trapezoid - Page 33

Shape B,E - Half Square Triangle - Page 17

Shape C - Rectangle - Page 18

Shape F - Square - Page 16

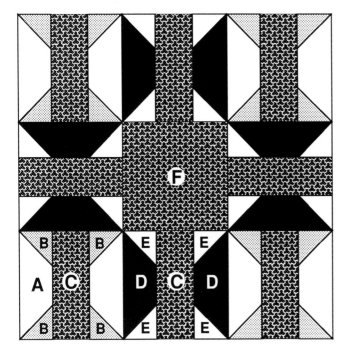

## CUTTING PROCEDURE:

A - Cut 1 - 1 7/8" x 44" (4.5 x 112cm) strip, light. Cut into eight 1 7/8" x 5 1/4" (4.5 x 12.7cm) rectangles. Recut into eight full trapezoids.

B - Cut 1 - 2 1/4" x 20" (5.2 x 51cm) strip, medium light. Cut into eight 2 1/4" (5.2cm) squares. Recut the squares in half diagonally.

C - Cut - 1 - 1 3/4" x 38" (4.2 x 96.5cm) strip, medium dark. Cut into eight 1 3/4" x 4 1/2" (4.2 x 11.2cm) rectangles.

D - Cut 1 - 1 7/8" x 44" (4.5 x 112cm) strip, dark. Cut into eight 1 7/8" x 5 1/4" (4.5 x 12.7cm) rectangles. Recut into eight full trapezoids.

E - Cut 1 - 2 1/4" x 20" (5.2 x 51cm) strip, light. Cut into eight 2 1/4" (5.2cm) squares. Recut the squares in half diagonally.

F - Cut 1 - 4 1/2" (11.2cm) square, medium dark.

## SEWING PROCEDURE:

1. Sew B to each side of A. Press to B. Make eight sets.

2. Following the diagram, sew an AB set to each side of C. Press to C. Make four units.

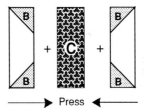

3. Sew E to each side of D. Press to D. Make eight sets.

4. Following the diagram, sew a DE set to each side of C. Press to C. Make four units.

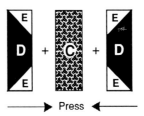

5. Butt, pin and sew into rows. Press according to the diagram.

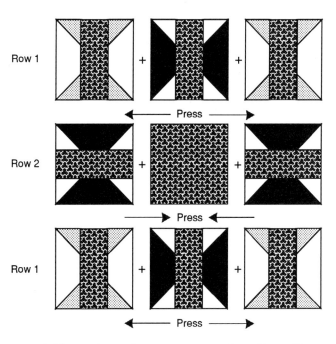

6. Butt, pin and sew rows together. Press Row 1 towards Row 2.

# BLAZING STAR

Block Size: 12" (30.5cm) square finished
Seam allowance: 1/4" (5mm)

Shapes Used In This Pattern and How To Cut Them:

Shape A,B,C - 45° Diamond - Page 21

Shape D - Half Square Triangle - Page 17

Shape E - Full Trapezoid - Page 33

Shape F - Clipped Square - Page 39

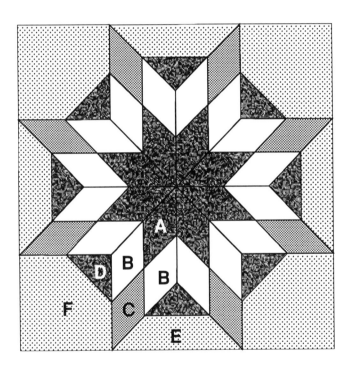

## CUTTING PROCEDURE:

A - Cut 1 - 1 3/4" x 26" (4.2 x 66cm) strip, dark.

B - Cut 2 - 1 3/4" x 26" (4.2 x 66cm) strips, light.

C - Cut 1 - 1 3/4" x 26" (4.2 x 66cm) strip, medium dark.

D - Cut 4 - 2 5/8" (6.2cm) squares, dark. Cut in half diagonally.

E - Cut 1 - 1 3/4" x 27" (4.2 x 69cm) strip, medium light. Cut into four 1 3/4" x 6 1/4" (4.2 x15.2cm) rectangles. Recut rectangles into four full trapezoids.

F - Cut 4 - 4" (9.9cm) squares, medium light. Position the ruler so the 1 1/2" (3.8cm) mark runs diagonally (corner to corner) on the square. Cut off the excess tip. See diagram.

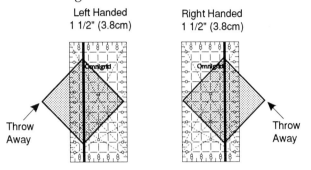

## SEWING PROCEDURE:

1. Pin the strips together according to the diagram. The strips are staggered 1 1/2" (3.8cm) in to allow for maximum use of fabric. Slowly sew SET 1 together. Press to A. Repeat for SET 2. Press SET 2 towards B.

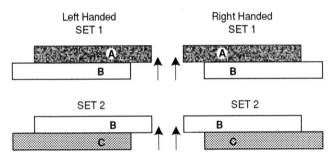

2. SET 1 - Using the 45° angle on the ruler as a guide, cut eight 1 3/4" (4.2cm) diagonal strips. Repeat for SET 2.

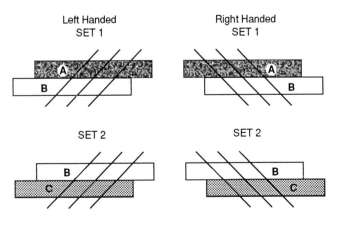

When you are cutting the 1 3/4" (4.2cm) strips make sure the 45° marking runs along the bottom of the strip and the ruler is 1 3/4" (4.2cm) in from the cut edge.

*NOTE: After cutting two 1 3/4" (4.2cm) diagonal strips, check to make sure you are still working with a 45° angle on your ruler.*

3. With the wrong side of AB strip facing you; match, pin and sew the recut diagonal strips together to form eight large diamonds. Press in the direction of the arrow. Cut off dog ears. See diagram.

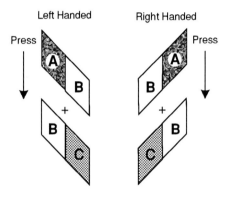

By pressing the seams in the direction shown, you will be able to butt all the seams together when sewing the eight large diamonds to form the Blazing Star.

4. Sewing the diamonds into pairs - Take two of the diamonds and pin together. Start sewing and stop 1/4" (5mm) from the bottom edge and back tack. Press according to the diagram. Cut off dog ears. Make four sets.

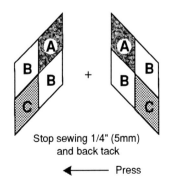

5. Sew two sets together to make a half. Remember to stop 1/4" (5mm) from the bottom edge and back tack. Repeat again for other half of the star. Press according to the diagram.

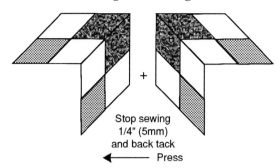

6. Butt and pin the two halves together. Start sewing 1/4" (5mm) in from the diamond edge, back tack, and stop 1/4" (5mm) from the end of the last diamond edge. Back tack. It doesn't matter which way you press the center seam.

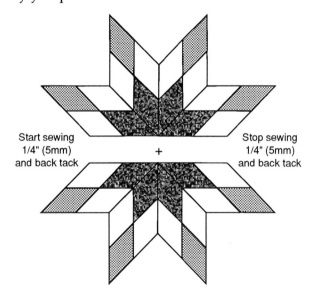

7. Sew D to E. Press to D. Cut off dog ears. Make four sets.

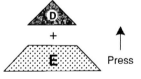

8. Sew D to F. Press to D. Cut off dog ears. Make four sets.

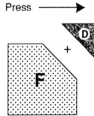

9. Sewing the DE triangle to the star - With the wrong side of the diamond facing you, pin to the correct side of the DE triangle. Start sewing from the outside tip of the diamond. Stop sewing when you reach the other seam and back tack.

Cut the thread and remove from the machine. Now with the wrong side of the DE triangle facing you, pin and sew to the diamond. Stop sewing when you reach the other seam and back tack. Press to DE. Do all four sides this way. Cut off all dog ears.

10. Sewing the DF square to the star - With the wrong side of the star facing you, pin to the correct side of the DF square. Start sewing. Stop sewing when you reach the other seam and back tack. Cut the thread and remove from the machine.

Now with the wrong side of DF square facing you, pin to the other diamond. Start sewing. Stop sewing when you reach the other seam and back tack. Press to DF. Do all four corners this way.

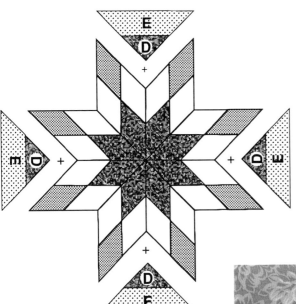

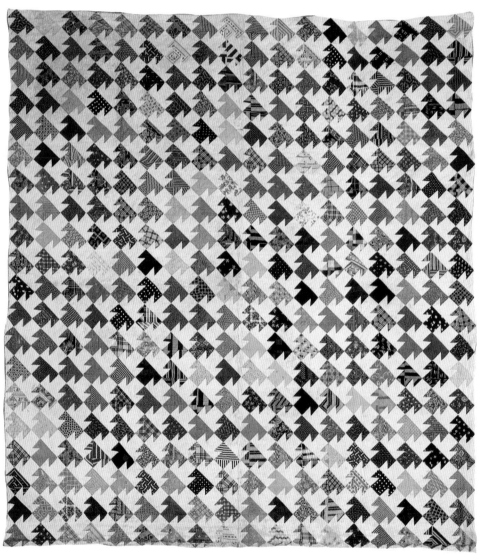

*Capital T Quilt from the collection of
Jeanne and Gene Wilber -
The Strawberry Patch Calico Shop*

# CAPITAL T

Block Size: 12" (30.5cm) square finished
Seam allowance: 1/4" (5mm)

Shapes Used In This Pattern and How To Cut Them:

Shape - A,D - Half Square Triangle - Page 17

Shape - B - Quarter Square Triangle - Page 18

Shape - C - Prism - Page 39

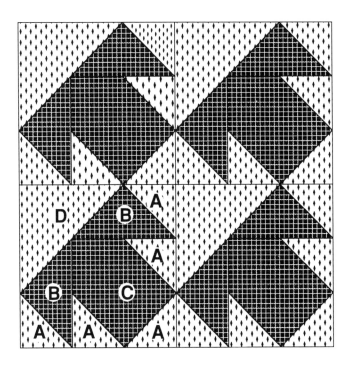

## CUTTING PROCEDURE:

A - Cut 10 - 3" (7.1cm) squares, light. Cut in half diagonally.

B - Cut 2 - 5 1/4" (12.7cm) squares, dark. Cut in half diagonally twice.

C - Cut 4 - 3 3/8" x 4 7/8" (8.3 x 12cm) rectangles, dark. Cut each into a prism shape.

D - Cut 2 - 4 7/8" (11.9cm) squares, light. Cut in half diagonally.

## SEWING PROCEDURE:

1. A is oversized. When sewing A to each side of C, make sure the same amount of dog ear hangs over each end. Make four sets. Press to A. Do not cut off dog ears.

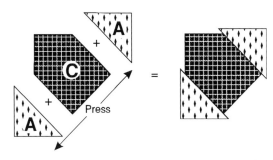

2. Sew A to the bottom of the AC set. Make sure the same amount of dog ear hangs over each end. Make four sets. Press to A.

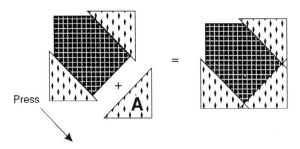

3. Square up the AC unit to measure 4 1/2" (11.2cm) square. Make sure you leave a 1/4" (5mm) seam allowance as the diagram shows.

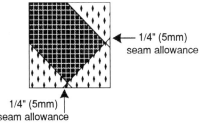

4. A is oversized. Sew A to the left side of B. The top will hang over the B point. Press to A. Make four sets.

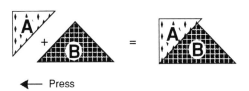

5. A is oversized. Sew A to the right side of B. The top will hang over the B point. Press to A. Make four sets.

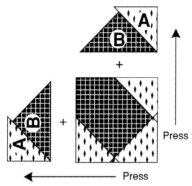

Press →

6. Following the diagram, add the proper AB unit to each side of the AC unit. Press seams to the AB unit.

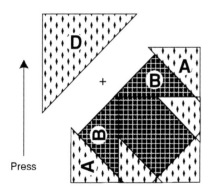

Press
← Press

7. D is oversized. When sewing D to the top of each ABC unit, make sure the same amount of dog ear hangs over each end. Press to D.

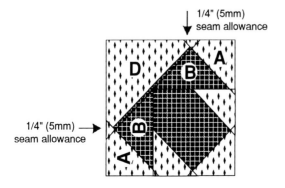

Press
+

8. Square up the block to measure 6 1/2" (16.2cm) square. Make sure you leave a 1/4" (5mm) seam allowance as the diagram shows.

1/4" (5mm) seam allowance

1/4" (5mm) → seam allowance

9. Butt, pin and sew into rows. Press according to the diagram.

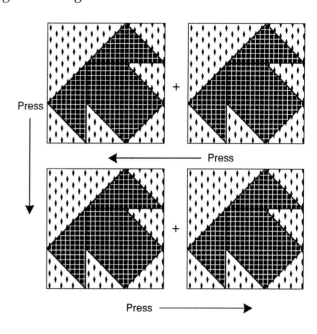

Press
+
← Press
+
Press →

---

140

# CONTRARY WIFE

Block Size: 12" (30.5cm) square finished
Seam allowance: 1/4" (5mm)

Shapes Used In This Pattern and How To Cut Them:

Shape A,B - Half Square Triangle - Page 17

Shape C,D,H - Square - Page 16

Shape E,F,G - Quarter Square Triangle - Page 18

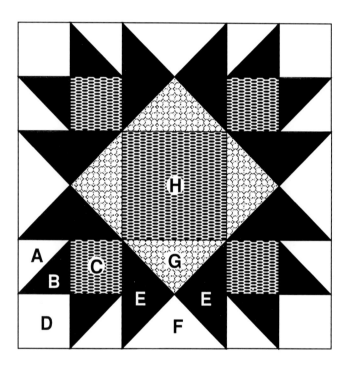

## CUTTING PROCEDURE:

A - Cut 4 - 2 7/8" (6.8cm) squares, light. Cut in half diagonally.

B - Cut 4 - 2 7/8" (6.8cm) squares, dark. Cut in half diagonally.

C - Cut 4 - 2 1/2" (6.1cm) squares, medium dark.

D - Cut 4 - 2 1/2" (6.1cm) squares, light.

E - Cut 2 - 5 1/4" (12.7cm) squares, dark. Cut in half diagonally twice.

F - Cut 1 - 5 1/4" (12.7cm) square, light. Cut in half diagonally twice.

G - Cut 1 - 5 1/4" (12.7cm) square, medium light. Cut in half diagonally twice.

H - Cut 1 - 4 1/2" (11.2cm) square, medium dark.

## SEWING PROCEDURE:

1. Sew A to B. Press to B. Make eight sets.

2. Sew one AB set to a C square. Press to C. Make two sets of each.

3. Sew one AB set to a D square. Press to D. Make two sets of each.

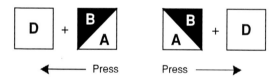

4. Butt, pin and sew one AB/C set to one AB/D set. Press to the AB/C set. Make two units of each.

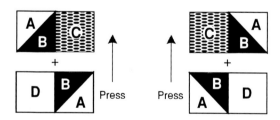

5. Sew E to F. Press to E. Make four sets. Sew E to G. Press to E. Make four sets.

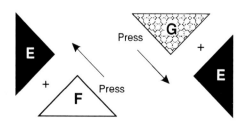

6. Sew one EF set to one EG set. Press to the EG set. Make four units.

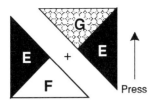

7. Pin and sew into rows following the diagram.

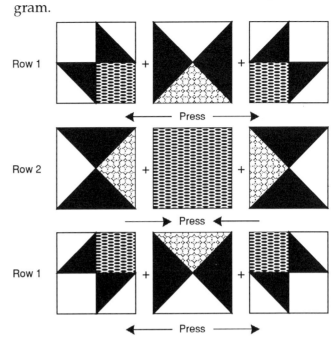

8. Butt, pin and sew Row 1 to Row 2. Add Row 1. Press to Row 2.

*Contrary Wife Quilt in the collection of Anita Bubul - Made by Carol Smith, Plains, Pa.*

# EIGHT POINTED STAR

Block Size: 12" (30.5cm) square finished
Seam allowance: 1/4" (5mm)

Shapes Used In This Pattern and How To Cut Them:

    Shape A - 45° Diamond - Page 21

    Shape B - Quarter Square Triangle - Page 18

    Shape C - Square - Page 16

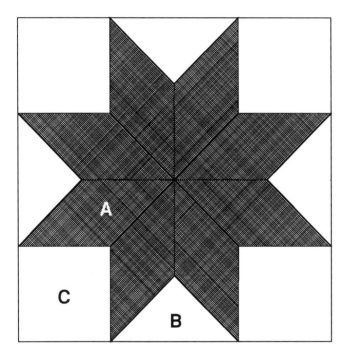

## CUTTING PROCEDURE:

    A - Cut 1 - 3" x 37" (7.4 x 94cm) strip, dark. Recut into eight 3" (7.4cm) 45° diamonds.

    B - Cut 1 - 6 1/4" (15.2cm) square, light. Cut in half diagonally twice.

    C - Cut 4 - 4" (9.9cm) squares, light.

## SEWING PROCEDURE:

    1. Sewing the diamonds into pairs - Take two of the diamonds and pin together. Start sewing and stop 1/4" (5mm) from the bottom edge and back

tack. Press according to the diagram. Cut off dog ears. Make four sets.

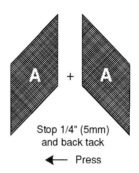

    2. Sew two sets together to make a half. Remember to stop 1/4" (5mm) from the bottom edge and back tack. Repeat again for other half of the star. Press according to the diagram.

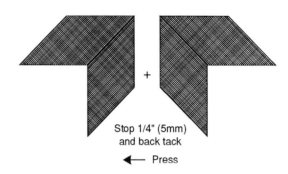

    3. Butt and pin the two halves together. Start sewing 1/4" (5mm) in from the diamond edge, back tack, and stop 1/4" (5mm) from the end of the last diamond edge. Back tack. It doesn't matter which way you press the center seam.

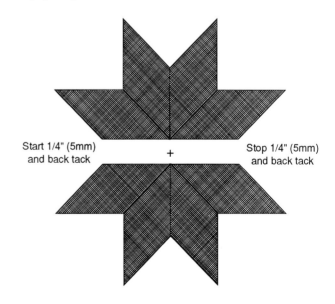

4. Sewing the B triangle to the star - With the wrong side of the diamond facing you, pin to the correct side of the B triangle. Start sewing from the outside tip of the diamond. Stop sewing when you reach the 1/4" (5mm) diamond seam and back tack.

Cut the thread and remove from the machine. Now with the wrong side of the B triangle facing you, pin and sew to the diamond. Stop sewing when you reach the 1/4" (5mm) diamond seam and back tack. Press to B. Do all four sides this way. Cut off all dog ears.

5. Sewing the C square to the star - With the wrong side of the star facing you, pin to the correct side of the C square. Start sewing. Stop sewing at the 1/4" (5mm) mark and back tack. Cut the thread and remove from the machine.

Now with the wrong side of C square facing you, pin to the other diamond. Start sewing. Stop sewing at the 1/4" (5mm) mark and back tack. Press to C. Do all four corners this way.

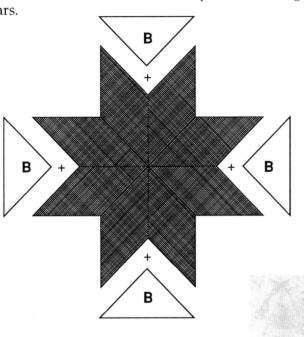

*NOTE: I cut a plastic template the same size as <u>one</u> of the A diamonds. I placed the template on flower fabric, drew around it and then rotary cut it.*

# FLYING SWALLOWS

Block Size: 12" (30.5cm) square finished
Seam allowance: 1/4" (5mm)

Shapes Used In This Pattern and How To Cut Them:

Shape A1, A2, A3 - 45° Diamond - Page 21

Shape B1, B2, B3, B4, C - Quarter Square Triangles - Page 18

Shape D - Square - Page 16

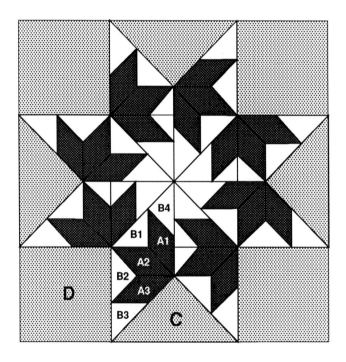

## CUTTING PROCEDURE:

A1, A2, A3 - Cut 2 - 1 9/16" x 31" (3.7 x 79cm) strips, medium dark. Position strips wrong sides together and cut into twenty-four 1 9/16" (3.7cm) 45° diamonds. (1 9/16" is located between 1 1/2" and 1 5/8")

B1, B2, B3, B4 - Cut 8 - 3 3/8" (7.9cm) squares, light. Cut in half diagonally twice.

C - Cut 1 - 6 1/4" (15.2cm) square, medium light. Cut in half diagonally twice.

D - Cut 4 - 4" (9.9cm) squares, medium light.

## SEWING PROCEDURE:

1. Start sewing A1 to A2 and stop 1/4" (5mm) from the bottom edge. Back tack. Press to A1. Do not clip the dog ear. Make eight sets.

Stop 1/4" (5mm)
and back tack
← Press

2. Dog ears will line up when sewing A2 to A3. Stop sewing 1/4" (5mm) from the bottom edge and back tack. Press to A2. Cut dog ears off. Repeat for all eight sets.

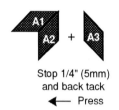

Stop 1/4" (5mm)
and back tack
← Press

3. With the wrong side of A1 diamond facing you, sew to the correct side of B1 triangle. Stop sewing when you reach the 1/4" (5mm) diamond seam and back tack. Cut the thread and remove from the machine.

Now with the wrong side of B1 triangle facing you, sew to A2 diamond. Stop sewing when you reach the 1/4" (5mm) diamond seam and back tack. Press to B1 triangle. Do not clip dog ears. Repeat for all eight sets.

4. With the wrong side of A2 diamond facing you, sew to the correct side of B2 triangle. Stop sewing when you reach the 1/4" (5mm) diamond seam and back tack. Cut the thread and remove from the machine.

Now with the wrong side of B2 triangle facing you, sew to A3 diamond. Stop sewing when you reach the 1/4" (5mm) diamond seam and back tack. Press to B2 triangle. Cut off dog ears.

Repeat for all eight sets.

5. Sew B3 and B4 triangles to complete the diamond unit. Press to B3 and B4. Cut off dog ears. Repeat for all eight sets.

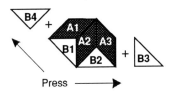

Press ⟶

6. Sewing the diamonds into pairs - Take two of the diamonds and pin together. Start sewing and stop 1/4" (5mm) from the bottom edge and back tack. Press according to the diagram. Cut off the dog ears. Make four sets.

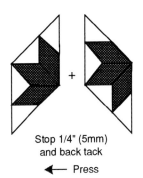

Stop 1/4" (5mm)
and back tack

◀— Press

7. Sew two sets together to make a half. Remember to stop 1/4" (5mm) from the bottom edge and back tack. Repeat again for other half of the star.

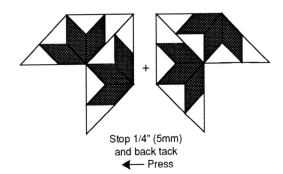

Stop 1/4" (5mm)
and back tack

◀— Press

8. Butt and pin the two halves together. Start sewing 1/4" (5mm) in from the diamond edge; back tack, and stopping 1/4" (5mm) from the end of the last diamond edge. Back tack. It doesn't matter which way you press the center seam.

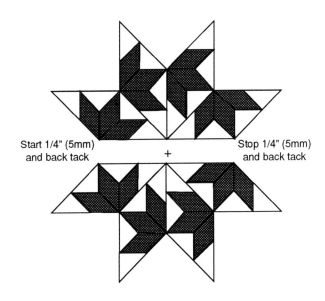

Start 1/4" (5mm)
and back tack

Stop 1/4" (5mm)
and back tack

9. Sewing the C triangle to the star - With the wrong side of the diamond facing you, pin to the correct side of the C triangle. Start sewing from the outside tip of the diamond. Stop sewing when you reach the 1/4" (5mm) diamond seam and back tack.

Cut the thread and remove from the machine. Now with the wrong side of the C triangle facing you, pin and sew to the diamond. Stop sewing when you reach the 1/4" (5mm) diamond seam and back tack. Press to C. Do all four sides this way. Cut off all dog ears.

10. Sewing the D square to the star - With the wrong side of the star facing you, pin to the correct side of the D square. Start sewing. Stop sewing at the 1/4" (5mm) mark and back tack. Cut the thread and remove from the machine.

Now with the wrong side of D square facing you, pin to the other diamond. Start sewing. Stop sewing at the 1/4" (5mm) mark and back tack. Press to D. Do all four corners this way.

# GOOSE TRACKS

Block Size: 12" (30.5cm) square finished
Seam allowance: 1/4" (5mm)

Shapes Used In This Pattern and How To Cut Them:

Shape A,B - Parallelogram  - Page 22

Shape C - Quarter Square Triangle - Page 18

Shape D,G - Square - Page 16

Shape E - Half Square Triangle - Page 17

Shape F - Rectangle - Page 18

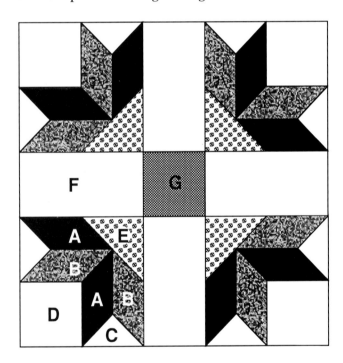

## CUTTING PROCEDURE:

A - Cut 1 - 1 3/4" x 32" (4.2 x 81cm) strip, dark. Right hand quilters cut with the right side of the fabric facing you. Left hand quilters cut with the wrong side of the fabric facing you. Make eight 2 1/4" (5.6cm) diagonal cuts.

B - Cut 1 - 1 3/4" x 32" (4.2 x 81cm) strip, medium dark. Right handed quilters will cut with the wrong side of the fabric fac-

ing you. Left hand quilters cut with the right side of the fabric facing you. Make eight 2 1/4" (5.6cm) diagonal cuts.

C - Cut 2 - 3 3/4" (8.9 cm) squares, light. Cut in half diagonally twice.

D - Cut 4 - 3" (7.4cm) squares, light.

E - Cut 2 - 3 3/8" (8.1cm), squares, medium. Cut in half diagonally.

F - Cut 4 - 2 1/2" x 5 1/2" (6.1 x 13.7cm) rectangles, light.

G - Cut 1 - 2 1/2" (6.1cm) square, medium.

## SEWING PROCEDURE:

1. Sew  A to B. Stop sewing 1/4" (5mm) from the bottom edge and back tack. Press to A. Cut dog ear off.  Make eight sets.

2. Sew two sets together.  Stop sewing 1/4" (5mm) from the bottom edge and back tack.  Press to B.  Make four units.

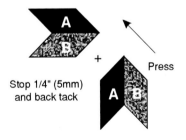

3. With the wrong side of A diamond facing you, sew to the correct side of C triangle.  Stop sewing when you reach the 1/4" (5mm) diamond seam and back tack.  Cut the thread and remove from the machine.

Now with the wrong side of C triangle facing you, sew to B diamond. Stop sewing when you reach the

1/4" (5mm) diamond seam and back tack. Press toward C. Cut off dog ears. Do this to all four units.

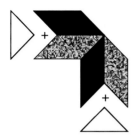

4. With the wrong side of B diamond facing you, pin to the correct side of the D square. Start sewing. Stop sewing at the 1/4" (5mm) mark and back tack. Cut the thread and remove from the machine.

Now with the wrong side of D square facing you, pin to the A diamond. Start sewing. Stop sewing at the 1/4" (5mm) mark and back tack. Press to D. Do this to all four units.

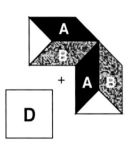

5. Sew E to the diamond unit. Press to E. Do this to all four units.

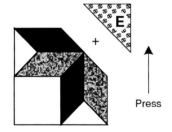

6. Pin and sew into rows. Press according to the diagram.

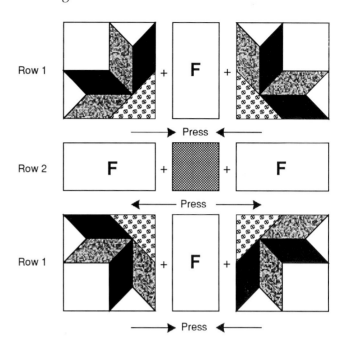

7. Press Row 1 towards Row 2.

# MEXICAN STAR

Block Size: 12" (30.5cm) square finished
Seam allowance: 1/4" (5mm)

Shapes Used In This Pattern and How To Cut
Them:

Shape A - Left Half Trapezoid - Page 35

Shape AR - Right Half Trapezoid - Page 35

Shape B - Quarter Square Triangle - Page 18

Shape C - Half Square Triangle - Page 17

Shape D,F - Square - Page 16

Shape E - Prism - Page 39

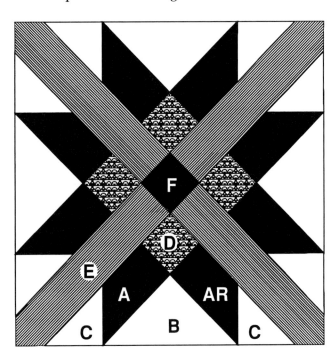

## CUTTING PROCEDURE:

A - Cut 1 - 2 1/8" x 20" (5.1 x 51cm) strip, dark. Cut into four 2 1/8" x 4 3/8" (5.1 x 10.6cm) rectangles. Left hand quilters cut with right side of the fabric facing you. Right hand quilters cut with the wrong side of the fabric facing you. Recut into four left half trapezoids.

AR -Cut 1 - 2 1/8" x 20" (5.1 x 51cm) strip, dark. Cut into four 2 1/8" x 4 3/8" (5.1 x 10.6cm) rectangles. Left hand quilters cut with the wrong side of the fabric facing you. Right hand quilters cut with the right side of the fabric facing you. Recut into four right half trapezoids.

B - Cut 1 - 6 1/4" (15.2cm) square, light. Cut in half diagonally twice.

C - Cut 4 - 3 1/4" (7.8cm) squares, light. Cut in half diagonally.

D - Cut 4 - 2 1/8" (5.1cm) squares, medium light.

E - Cut 1 - 2 1/4" x 35" (5.4 x 89cm) strip, medium dark. Cut into four 2 1/4" x 8 3/8" (5.4 x 20.9cm) rectangles. Recut each into a prism shape.

F - Cut 1 - 2 1/4" (5.4cm) square, dark.

## SEWING PROCEDURE:

1. Sew A to B. Press to A. Cut dog ear off. Make four sets.

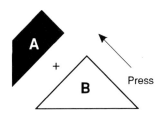

2. Sew D to AR. Press to AR. Make four sets.

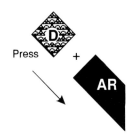

3. Butt, pin and sew the DAR set to the AB set. Press to the DAR set. Cut dog ear off.

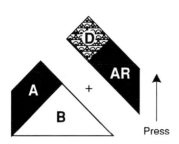

4. Sew C to each side of the AB/DAR set. Press to C. Cut dog ears off. Make four units.

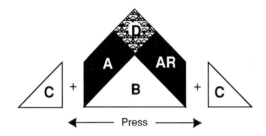

5. Butt, pin and sew a side unit to each side of E. Press to E. Make two sets.

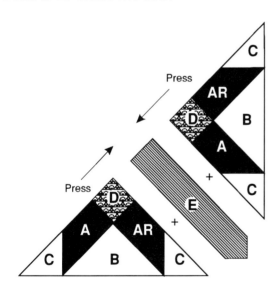

6. Sew E to each side of F. Press to E.

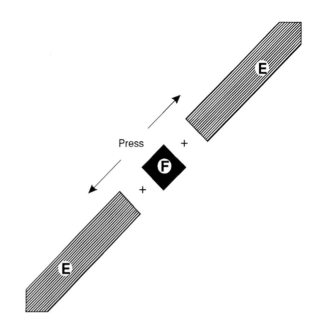

7. Following the diagram, butt, pin and sew together. Press to the EF strip.

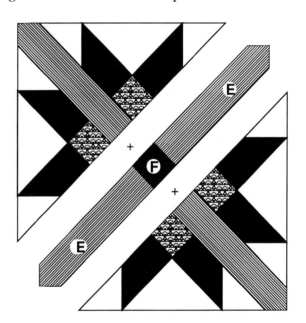

*Mexican Star*

*Morning Star*

# MORNING STAR

Block Size: 12" (30.5cm) square finished
Seam allowance: 1/4" (5mm)

Shapes Used In This Pattern and How To Cut Them:

Shape A,H - Square - Page 16

Shape B - Right Half Trapezoid - Page 35

Shape C - Left Half Trapezoid - Page 35

Shape D - Half Square Triangle - Page 17

Shape E,F - Parallelogram - Page 22

Shape G - Quarter Square Triangle - Page 18

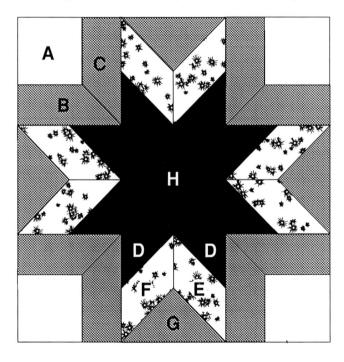

## CUTTING PROCEDURE:

A - Cut 4 - 3 1/2" (8.6cm) squares, light.

B - Cut 4 - 1 7/8" x 5 1/8" (4.5 x 12.5cm) rectangles, medium dark. Left hand quilters cut with the wrong side of the fabric facing you. Right hand quilters cut with the right side of the fabric facing you. Recut into four right half trapezoids.

C - Cut 4 - 1 7/8" x 5 1/8" (4.5 x 12.5cm) rectangles, medium dark. Left hand quilters cut with the right side of the fabric facing you. Right hand quilters cut with the wrong side of the fabric facing you. Recut into four left half trapezoids.

D - Cut 4 - 2 15/16" (7cm) squares, dark. (2 15/16" is located between 2 7/8" and 3") Cut in half diagonally.

E - Cut 1 - 2 1/2" x 14" (6.1 x 36cm) strip, medium light.

F - Cut 1 - 2 1/2" x 14" (6.1 x 36cm) strip, medium light.

Position the E strip on top of the F strip, wrong sides together. With the right side facing you, make four 1 15/16" (4.6cm) diagonal cuts. (1 15/16" is located between 1 7/8" and 2").Separate the parallelograms and you will have four Es and four Fs.

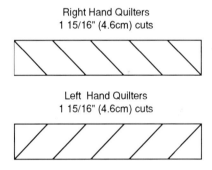

G - Cut 1 - 5 1/4" (12.7cm) square, dark. Cut in half diagonally twice.

H - Cut 1 - 4 1/2" ( 11.2cm) square, dark.

## SEWING PROCEDURE:

1. Pin B to C right sides together. With the wrong side of B facing you, start sewing and stop 1/4" (5mm) from the edge and back tack. Do not press.

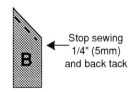

Stop sewing 1/4" (5mm) and back tack

2. Pin one side of A to the BC block. With the wrong side of C facing you, start sewing. Stop sewing when you reach the diagonal stitching of the BC block and back tack. Cut the thread and remove from the machine.

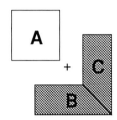

3. Pin the other side of A square to B. With the A piece facing you, start sewing and stop when you reach the other stitching line. Press to the BC section. Make four sets.

4. The ABC block is oversized. Trim so A is 3" (7.5cm) square and BC are 1 1/2" wide x 4 1/2" (3.7 x 11.2cm) long. The block now measures 4 1/2" (11.2cm) square.

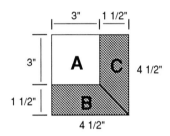

5. Pin E to F right sides together. With the wrong side of E facing you, start sewing and stop 1/4" (5mm) from the edge and back tack. Press to F. Make four sets.

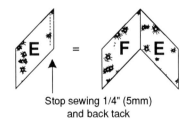

6. Sew D to the EF set. Press to D. Trim dog ears. Make four sets.

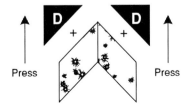

7. Pin F to G. With the wrong side of F facing you, start sewing. Stop sewing when you reach the straight stitching line of EF and back tack. Cut the thread and remove from the machine.

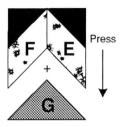

8. Pin E to G. With the wrong side of G facing you, start sewing. Stop sewing when you reach the other stitching line and back tack. Press to G. Trim dog ears. This section will measure 4 1/2" (11.2cm) Make four sets.

9. Pin and sew into rows. Press according to the diagram.

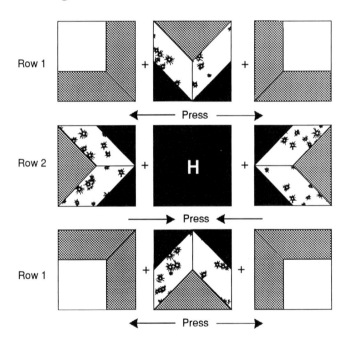

10. Press Row 1 towards Row 2.

154

# QUEEN'S COURTYARD

Block Size: 12" (30.5cm) square finished
Seam allowance: 1/4" (5mm)

Shapes Used In This Pattern and How To Cut Them:

Shape A,B,C - Kite - Page 36

Shape D - Half Square Triangle - Page 17

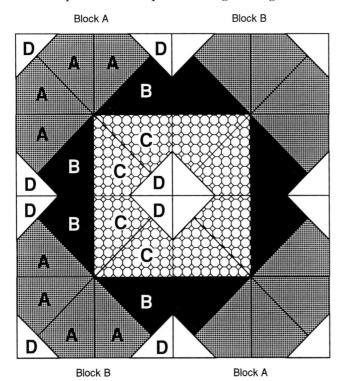

Block A          Block B

Block B          Block A

## CUTTING PROCEDURE:

A - Cut 8 - 3 7/8" (9.4cm) squares, medium dark. Cut in half diagonally. Recut into sixteen kite shapes.

B - Cut 4 - 3 7/8" (9.4cm) squares, dark. Cut in half diagonally. Recut into eight kite shapes.

C - Cut 4 - 3 7/8" (9.4cm) squares, medium light. Cut in half diagonally. Recut into eight kite shapes.

D - Cut 8 - 2 3/4" (6.5cm) squares, light. Cut in half diagonally. (These pieces are slightly oversized. You will "square up" after sewing).

## SEWING PROCEDURE FOR BLOCK A:

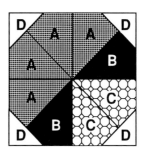

1. Bottom of The Block - Following the diagram, sew B to A. Press to A. Sew C to another C. Press to the correct C. Cut dog ears off. Make two sets.

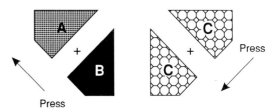

2. Top of The Block - Following the diagram, sew A to B. Press to B. Sew A to another A. Press to the correct A. Cut dog ears off. Make two sets.

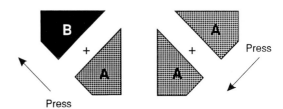

3. Sew the AB set to the CC set. Press to the AB set. Sew the BA set to the AA set. Press to the BA set. Make two units.

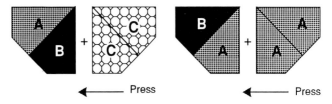

4. Butt, pin and sew the two halves together. Repeat for the other two halves. Press to the AAAB unit.

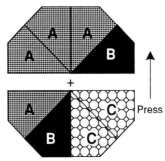

---

155

5. Sew a D triangle on the proper corners. Press these seams **in** towards the block. If necessary, square up D triangles.

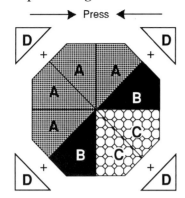

## Sewing Procedure For Block B:

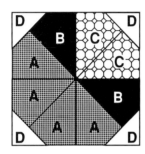

6. Bottom of The Block - Following the diagram, sew A to A. Press to the correct A. Sew B to A. Press to A. Cut dog ears off. Make two sets.

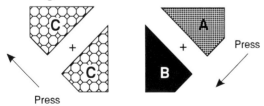

7. Top of The Block - Following the diagram, sew C to C. Press to the correct C. Sew A to B. Press to B. Cut dog ears off. Make two sets.

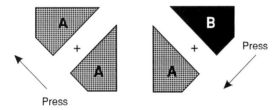

8. Sew the AA set to the BA set. Press to the AA set. Sew the CC set to the AB set. Press to the CC set. Make two units.

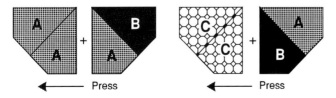

9. Butt, pin and sew the two halves together. Repeat for the other two halves. Press to the ABCC unit.

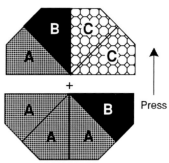

10. Sew a D triangle on the proper corners. Press these seams OUT from the block. If necessary, square up D triangles.

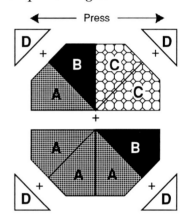

11. Row 1 - Butt, pin and sew block A to block B. Press to block A. Repeat for Row 2.

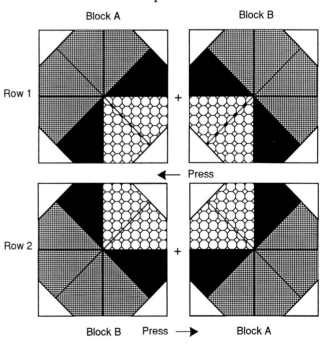

12. Butt, pin and sew Row 1 to Row 2. It doesn't matter which way you press the center seam.

# SUNRISE STAR

Block Size: 12" (30.5cm) square finished
Seam allowance: 1/4" (5mm)

Shapes Used In This Pattern and How To Cut Them:

Shape A - Kite - Page 36

Shape B,C - Quarter Square Triangle - Page 18

Shape D - Half Square Triangle - Page 17

Shape E - Octagon - Page 28

Shape F - Square - Page 16

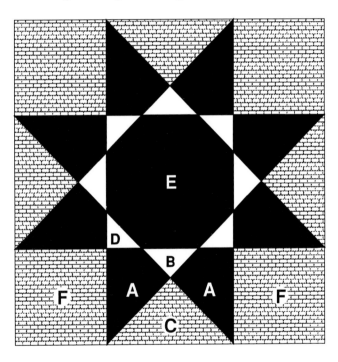

## CUTTING PROCEDURE:

A - Cut 4 - 4 3/8" (10.6cm) squares, dark. Place 2 squares, wrong sides together. Cut in half. Recut into the kite shape. Repeat with the other two squares.

B - Cut 1 - 3 1/4" (7.6cm) square, light. Cut in half diagonally twice.

C - Cut 1 - 6 1/4" (15.2cm) square, medium light. Cut in half diagonally twice.

D - Cut 2 - 2 3/8" (5.6cm) squares, light. Cut in half diagonally.

E - Cut 1 - 5 1/2" (13.7cm) square, dark. Cut into an octagon.

F - Cut 4 - 4" (9.9cm) squares, medium light.

## SEWING PROCEDURE:

1. Sew A to B. Press to B. Cut off the dog ear. Make four sets.

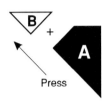

2. Sew A to C. Press to C. Cut off the dog ear. Make four sets.

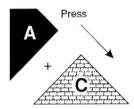

3. Sew the AB section to the AC section. Press to the AB section. Cut off the dog ear. Make four sets.

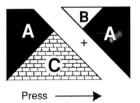

4. Sew D to the four corners of E. Press to D.

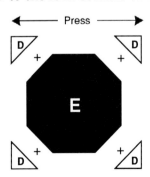

5. Pin and sew into rows. Press according to the diagram.

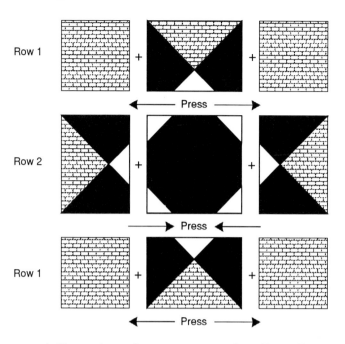

6. Butt, pin and sew rows together. Press Row 2 towards Row 1.

# SWING IN THE CENTER

Block Size: 12" (30.5cm) square finished
Seam allowance: 1/4" (5mm)

Shapes Used In This Pattern and How To Cut Them:

Shape A,D - Quarter Square Triangle - Page 18

Shape B,C - Half Square Triangle - Page 17

Shape E - Prism - Page 39

Shape F,G - Square - Page 16

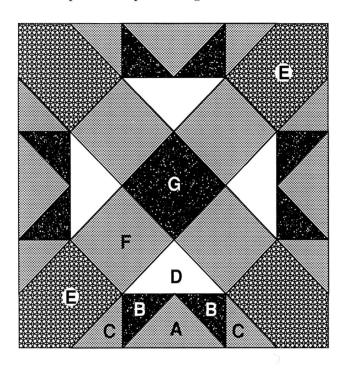

## CUTTING PROCEDURE:

A - Cut 1 - 5 1/4" (12.7cm) square, medium light. Cut in half diagonally twice.

B - Cut 4 - 2 7/8" (6.8cm) squares, dark. Cut in half diagonally.

C - Cut 4 - 2 7/8" (6.8cm) squares, medium light. Cut in half diagonally.

D - Cut 1 - 5 1/4" (12.7cm) square, light. Cut in half diagonally twice.

E - Cut 4 - 3 5/16" x 4 7/8" (8.1 x 12cm) rectangles, medium dark. (3 5/16" is located between 3 1/4" and 3 3/8"). Cut each into the prism shape.

F - Cut 4 - 3 5/16" (8.1cm) squares, medium light. (3 5/16" is located between 3 1/4" and 3 3/8").

G - Cut 1 - 3 5/16" (8.1cm) square, dark. (3 5/16" is located between 3 1/4" and 3 3/8").

## SEWING PROCEDURE:

1. Sew B to each side of A. Press to B. Cut off the dog ears. Make four sets.

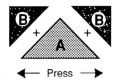

2. Sew C to each side of the AB set. Press to C. Cut off the dog ears. Make four sets.

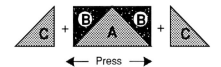

3. Sew D to the ABC set. Press to D. Cut off the dog ears. Make four units.

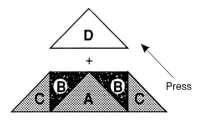

4. Sew E to F. Press to E. Make two sets.

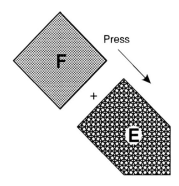

5. Sew an ABCD unit to each side of the EF set. Press to the EF section. Make two units.

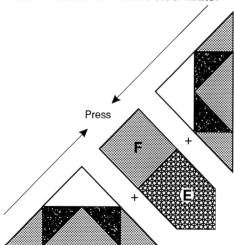

7. Sew the side units to the EFG strip. Press to the EFG strip.

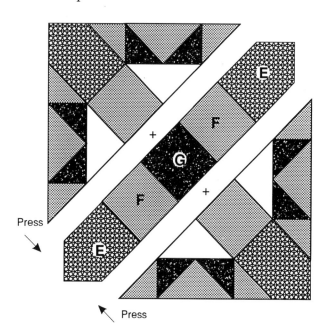

6. Following the diagram, sew the center strip together. Press away from G, the center square. Make one strip.

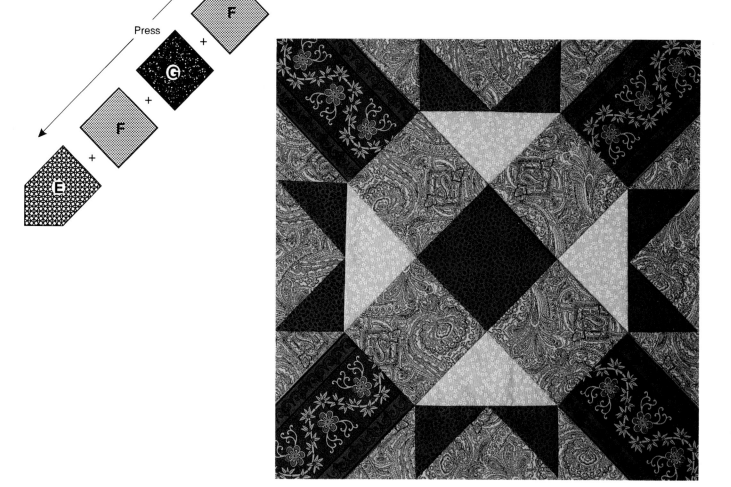

*Grandmother's Flower Garden Quilt*

# GRANDMA'S FLOWER GARDEN

Each Hexagon Size: 2" (5.1cm) finished
Seam allowance: 1/4" (5mm)

Shape Used In This Pattern and How To Cut It:

Shape A,B,C - Hexagon - Page 26

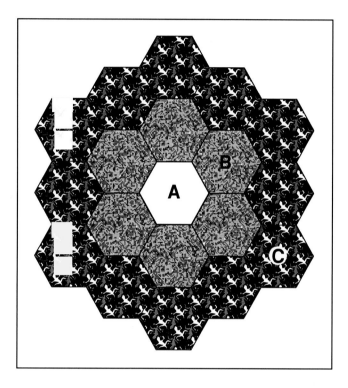

## GENERAL INFORMATION FOR SEWING HEXAGONS

Start sewing in from the edge 1/4"(5mm), back tack and stop sewing 1/4" (5mm) from the other edge. Back tack.

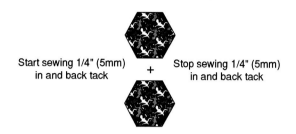

Start sewing 1/4" (5mm) in and back tack       Stop sewing 1/4" (5mm) in and back tack

## SEWING PROCEDURE:

1. Following the diagram below, sew into rows. Remember to start in 1/4" (5mm) from the edge, back tack and stop 1/4" (5mm) from the other edge. Back tack.

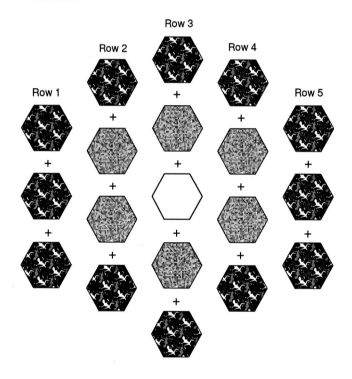

Row 1   Row 2   Row 3   Row 4   Row 5

## CUTTING PROCEDURE:

A - Cut 1 - 2 1/2" x 6" (6.1 x 15cm) strip, light. Cut into one 2 1/2" (6.1cm) - 60° diamond. Recut into a hexagon.

B - Cut 1 - 2 1/2" x 20" (6.1 x 51cm) strip, medium light. Cut into six 2 1/2" (6.1cm) - 60° diamonds. Recut into six hexagons.

C - Cut 1 - 2 1/2" x 44" (6.1 x 111.8cm) strip, dark. Cut into twelve 2 1/2" (6.1cm) - 60° diamonds. Recut into twelve hexagons.

2. To sew Row 1 to Row 2 - With the wrong side of Row 2 facing you, start sewing the correct sides together. Stop sewing when you reach the other stitching line. Back tack.

Flip the rows so you have the wrong side of Row 1 facing you. You will now see two lines of stitching. Start sewing between the two lines of stitching, back tack and continue sewing until you reach the other stitching line. Back tack.

Flip the rows so you have the wrong side of Row 2 facing you. You will again see two lines of stitching. Start sewing between the two lines of stitching, back tack and continue sewing until you reach the other stitching line. Back tack.

Continue sewing Row 1 to Row 2 by flipping the rows every other time. Remember - You will know you are doing it correctly because you will always be sewing between two stitching lines. The only time you won't be sewing between two stitching lines is at the very beginning seam and at the very end seam.

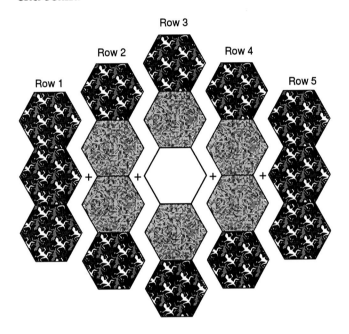

3. Sewing Row 2 to Row 3 - With the wrong side of Row 3 facing you, start sewing the correct sides together. Stop sewing when you reach the other stitching line. Back tack.

Flip the rows so you have the wrong side of Row 2 facing you. You will now see two lines of stitching. Start sewing between the two lines of stitching, back tack and continue sewing until you reach the other stitching line. Back tack.

Flip the rows so you have the wrong side of Row 3 facing you. You will again see two lines of stitching. Start sewing between the two lines of stitching, back tack and continue sewing until you reach the other stitching line. Back tack.

Continue sewing Row 2 to Row 3 by flipping the rows every other time.

4. Sewing Row 3 to Row 4 - With the wrong side of Row 3 facing you, start sewing the correct sides together. Stop sewing when you reach the other stitching line. Back tack.

Flip the rows so you have the wrong side of Row 4 facing you, you will see the two lines of stitching. Start sewing between the two lines of stitching, back tack and continue sewing until you reach the other stitching line. Back tack.

Now flip the rows so Row 3 is facing you. Start sewing between the two lines of stitching, back tack and continue sewing until you reach the other stitching line. Back tack.

Continue flipping the rows every other time.

5. Sewing Row 5 to Row 4 - With the wrong side of Row 4 facing you, start sewing the correct sides together. Stop sewing when you reach the other stitching line. Back tack.

Flip the rows so you have the wrong side of Row 5 facing you, you will see the two lines of stitching. Start sewing between the two lines of stitching, back tack and continue sewing until you reach the other stitching line. Back tack.

Continue flipping the rows every other time.

6. Pressing - This is the only block I press on the wrong side when I am finished. Carefully press the seams whichever way you want them to go. You be the judge.

To make a quilt from this pattern - Make the required number of flowers. Cut the required number of white or green hexagons for the garden path. Sew the white or green hexagons to the flowers in rows. Sew the rows together.

This is the easiest method I have developed to put together a Grandma's Flower Garden Quilt or Miniature.

# SIX POINTED STAR

Block Size: 11 3/4" height (29.8cm) hexagon, finished

Seam allowance: 1/4" (5mm)

Shape Used In This Pattern and How To Cut It:

Shape A,B,C,D - 60° Diamond - Page 24

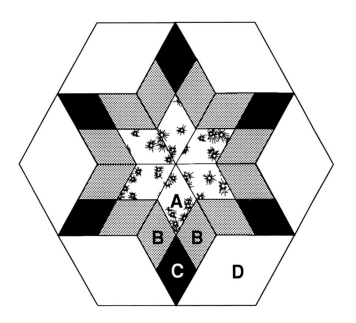

## Cutting Procedure:

A - Cut 1 - 2" x 17" (4.8 x 43.2cm) strip, medium light.

B - Cut 2 - 2" x 17" (4.8 x 43.2cm) strips, medium dark.

C - Cut 1 - 2" x 17" (4.8 x 43.2cm) strip, dark.

D - Cut 1 - 3 1/2" x 27" (8.6 x 69cm) strip, light. Cut into six 3 1/2" (8.6cm) 60° diamonds.

## Sewing Procedure:

1. Pin the strips together according to the diagram. The strips are staggered 1 1/2" (3.8cm) in to allow for maximum use of fabric. Slowly sew SET 1 together. Press to A. Repeat for SET 2. Press SET 2 towards B.

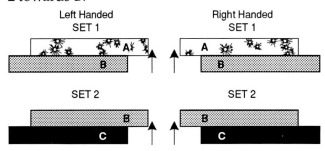

2. Using the 60 ° angle on the ruler as a guide, cut six 2" (4.8cm) diagonal strips. Repeat for SET 2 and SET 3.

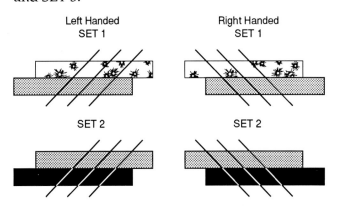

When you are cutting the 2" (4.8cm) strips make sure the 60° marking runs along the bottom of the strip and the ruler is 2" (4.8cm) in from the cut edge.

NOTE: *After cutting two 2" (4.8cm) diagonal strips, check to make sure you are still working with a 60° angle.*

3. With the wrong side of AB piece facing you, match, pin and sew the recut diagonal strips together to form six large diamonds. Press in the direction of the arrow. Cut off dog ears.

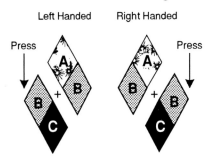

By pressing the seams in the direction shown, you will be able to butt all the seams together when sewing the six large diamonds to form the star.

4. To Make Half A Star - Butt, pin and sew two large diamonds together. Stop sewing 1/4" (5mm) from the bottom and back tack. Press according to the diagram. Do not cut the dog ear off.

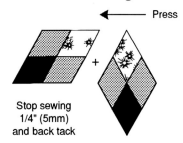

Press ←

Stop sewing
1/4" (5mm)
and back tack

5. Butt, pin and sew another large diamond to this unit. Stop sewing 1/4" (5mm) from the bottom and back tack. Press according to the diagram. Cut the dog ears off. You now have half a star. Repeat for the other half of the star.

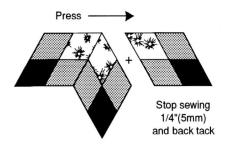

Press →

+

Stop sewing
1/4"(5mm)
and back tack

6. Sewing The Two Halves Together - Butt and pin the two halves, together. Start sewing 1/4" (5mm) in from the diamond edge, back tack, and stop 1/4" (5mm) from the end of the last diamond edge. Back tack. It doesn't matter which way you press the center seam.

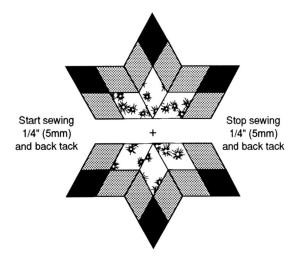

Start sewing
1/4" (5mm)
and back tack

+

Stop sewing
1/4" (5mm)
and back tack

7. Sewing D Diamonds To The Star - With the wrong side of the star facing you, pin to the correct side of a D diamond. Start sewing from the outside tip of the star. Stop sewing when you reach the other 1/4" (5mm) seam and back tack.

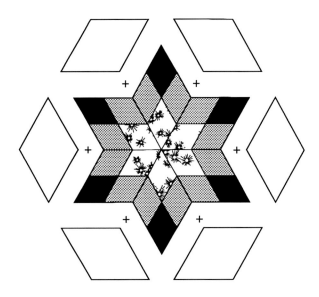

Cut the thread and remove from the machine. Now with the wrong side of the D diamond facing you, pin and sew to the star. Stop sewing when you reach the other 1/4" (5mm) diamond seam and back tack. Press seams to the D diamond. Do all six D diamonds this way. Cut off all dog ears.

# MIGRATION

*(COPYRIGHT 1991 NANCY JOHNSON-SREBRO)*

Size: 62 1/2" square, quilted
Seam allowance: 1/4"

Shapes Used In This Pattern and How To Cut Them:

Shape A,C - Quarter Square Triangle - Page 18

Shape B,E - Half Square Triangle - Page 17

Shape D - Square - Page 16

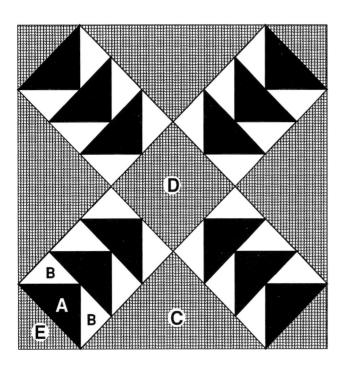

## CUTTING PROCEDURE
## TO MAKE ONE 4″ BLOCK:

A - Cut 1 - 2 1/4" x 7" strip, dark. Cut into three 2 1/4" squares. Recut squares in half diagonally twice.

B - Cut 1 - 1 1/2" x 20" strip, light. Cut into twelve 1 1/2" squares. Recut squares in half diagonally. These pieces are slightly oversized.

C - Cut 1 - 3 1/4" square, medium light. Cut in half diagonally twice.

D - Cut 1 - 1 3/8" square, medium light.

E - Cut 2 - 1 3/4" squares, medium light. Cut in half diagonally. These pieces are slightly oversized.

## SEWING PROCEDURE:

1. Sew one B to the side of A. Press to B. Add another B to the other side of A. Press to B. Make twelve geese.

2. After sewing and pressing, trim the top of the block to within 1/4" of the goose. Your geese will now measure 15/16" x 1 3/8".

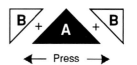

3. Sew three geese together to form a row. Make four rows.

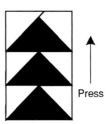

4. Sew one C to each side of a row of geese. Press to C. Due to minor differences in sewing and cutting, some students use a scant 1/4" seam allowance for steps 4 through 6. You be the judge. Make two sets. These are the sides of the block.

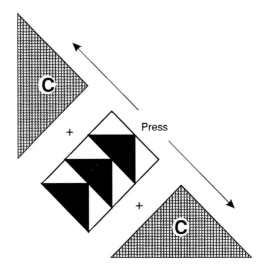

5. Sew D to two rows of geese. Press to D. This is the center of the block.

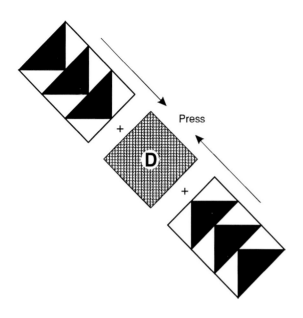

6. Sew the side sections (ABC) to the center section (ABD). Press to the side sections (ABC). Sew one E to each corner. Press towards E. "Square Up" E if necessary. (Don't forget to leave the 1/4" seam allowance when you "square up"). Measure your block. My block measured 4" square.

7. Make 33 flying geese blocks for the center section. Study the center section of the colored photo of this quilt. You will notice each flying geese block requires three colors. I used three different colors in each block for a total of 99 different fabrics and colors. Also for a real scrappy look, some of the blocks have dark geese with light background; and some have light geese with dark background.

**OUTSIDE BORDER:**
Cut 4 - 4 1/4" x 70" strips, medium light. Cut to the desired length later. Use the left over fabric to cut the solid squares and cornerstones.

**SOLID SQUARES:**
F - Cut 48 squares, medium light the size of your block. (Mine were 4" x 4" squares).

**LATTICE STRIPS:**
Cut 144 - 1" x the size of your block, dark. (Mine were 1" x 4" lattice strips).

**CORNERSTONE:**
Cut 64 - 1" x 1" squares, medium light.

**SEWING PROCEDURE FOR THE CENTER SECTION:**
8. Refering to the colored photo on page 171, sew into rows.

**PRESSING PROCEDURE FOR THE CENTER SECTION:**
9. Press the rows containing lattice strips and solid blocks towards the lattice strips.

Press the rows containing lattice strips and cornerstones towards the lattice strips.

Press the rows containing solid blocks, lattice strips, and flying geese blocks towards the lattice strips.

10. Butt, pin and sew rows together. Press to the rows containing the lattice strips and cornerstones.

After making the center section, I made the four side sections. Then I was able to determine how wide to make the inner border.

# SIDE SECTION:

Shapes Used in This Pattern and How To Cut Them:

Shape F, M, N - Quarter Square Triangle - Page 18

Shape G, H, O - Half Square Triangle - Page 17

Shape I, J, K, L - Square - Page 16

## CUTTING PROCEDURE FOR ONE SIDE SECTION:

F - Cut 21 - 3 3/8" squares, medium light. Cut in half diagonally twice.

G - Cut 84 - 2" squares, dark. Cut in half diagonally.

H - Cut 12 - 1 15/16" squares, dark. Cut in half diagonally. (1 15/16" is located between 1 7/8" and 2").

I - Cut 6 - 2" squares, contrasting medium light.

J - Cut 6 - 2 5/8" squares, medium light.

K - Cut 4 - 3 3/4" squares, medium light.

L - Cut 5 - 3 3/4" squares, contrasting medium light.

M - Cut 2 - 5 3/4" squares, medium light. Cut in half diagonally twice. You will use six triangles per side section.

N - Cut 2 - 4 1/4" squares, medium light. Cut in half diagonally twice.

O - Cut 1 - 1 - 3 1/4" square, medium light. Cut in half diagonally. You will use one triangle per section.

## SEWING PROCEDURE:

11. Sew one G to the side of G. Press to G. Add another G to the other side of F. Press to G. If necessary. trim the top of the block to within 1/4" of the goose as in step 2. Make eighty-four geese.

12. Sew two Hs to the opposite sides of I. Press to H. Add H to the other two sides. Press to H. Make six squares.

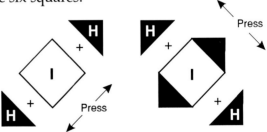

13. Following the Side Section diagram, sew the appropriate blocks into rows.

14. Row 1: Press seams towards N, J, H/I, blocks.

Row 2: Press seams towards K, L, M blocks.

15. Butt, pin and sew rows together. Press these seams towards Row 2.

16. Following the cutting procedure, sewing procedure and color photo of Migration, piece the other three side sections. **Give special attention to what direction the geese fly in.**

### INNER BORDER
Measure the center section. Mine measured 38" square. If your center section does not measure the same as mine, you will have to adjust the length and width of the inner border so the side sections will fit.

The width of my inner border was 2".

### OUTSIDE BORDER
Measure the quilt. Cut borders to the desired length and sew to the quilt.

### YARDAGE FOR MIGRATION
99 different scraps of light, medium and dark for the small geese.

4 yards medium light for outside border, inside border, solid squares, cornerstones, F, J, K, M, N, O.

1 3/4 yards dark for lattice strips, G, H.

1/2 yard contrasting medium light for I, L.

*Migration ©*

# QUESTIONS AND ANSWERS

The following are the questions I am asked most frequently when lecturing. Most of these questions touch on topics I covered extensively in **Miniature to Masterpiece©**, so I will not go in depth with a lot of detail.

**Q.** How much fabric do you buy?
**A.** I usually buy either 1 yard pieces or 10 yard pieces.

**Q.** Why the big difference in yardages?
**A.** I use only small bits of the 1 yard pieces in my miniatures and full size miniature quilts. The 10 yard pieces are usually of background prints or fabrics I can't live without. I may not be able to use them for a year or two but I will have them on hand when I need them.

**Q.** How much money do you spend on fabric and what does your husband say?
**A.** I have been known to spend $5,000.00 a year on fabric. My husband gave up on me years ago! He is still trying to figure out how I spend so much money on fabric when I work in miniatures.

**Q.** What type of batting do you use?
**A.** Mountain Mist Batting is still my favorite.

**Q.** What type of sewing machine do you use?
**A.** I use a 21 year old White™ sewing machine.

**Q.** What type of sewing machine will you buy when this one breaks?
**A.** I don't know. I keep hoping I won't have to face that situation. I do know that when I look for a machine, I will take 1/4" masking tape, a size 11 needle, my special fine silk pins and some 100% cotton pieces with me. When trying out the sewing machine, I will actually make a quilt block. That is the only smart way to determine what sewing machine is going to meet your quilting needs.

**Q.** Which are your favorite colors?
**A.** I would probably have to say red, tan, black and blue.

**Q.** How do you come up with your ideas?
**A.** That's a hard question. I'd like to think that a lot of my talent is **God** given. I have been fortunate enough to have a supportive family who understands my feelings about quiltmaking. With their support, I am allowed the time I need to play around with ideas, visit other Guilds for stimulation and meet once a month with a group of special quilting

friends. From this interaction I am then able to come up with my ideas. I don't know any other way to describe it. It just happens. But not without a lot of tears!

**Q.** Do you cry easily over your quilts?
**A.** Only when I'm working on them. Never afterwards.

**Q.** Do you always use 100% cotton?
**A.** Yes. It works the best for me.

**Q.** Do you wear a thimble when you quilt?
**A.** Yes, a metal thimble but because of my hands I do very limited quilting.

**Q.** What size quilting needle do you use?
**A.** I use a size 10 needle.

**Q.** Do you find working with a three color quilt stimulating?
**A.** No. The more colors and fabrics the better.

**Q.** You like working on scrap quilts?
**A.** Yes, but when I say scraps, I don't mean a hodgepodge of colors. I usually work with 50 to 300 different fabrics (not colors) in my full size miniature quilts; and you will notice I work in a color theme. Once I have chosen three or four main colors, I work in lots of shades of those colors.

**Q.** Where do you get your quilting designs from?
**A.** I have always liked Shirley Thompson's and Pepper Cory's design quilting motifs books. The last four years my good friend and quilter, Debbie Grow and I have collaborated on our own designs.

**Q.** How long did it take you to make one of your Masterpiece Quilts?
**A.** Longer than I care to remember! About 500 hours of work goes into each quilt. (That's roughly 8 hours every day for 2 months)

**Q.** How long does it take Debbie to quilt a full size miniature quilt?
**A.** It takes anywhere from 500 - 700 hours to complete the quilting.

**Q.** What type of binding does Debbie use?
**A.** I'm proud to say, I put the binding on my quilts. I use a double French Binding. The binding is cut on the crossgrain; not the bias! It is much easier to handle when not cut on the bias. Plus you waste so much fabric cutting on the bias.

# Other quiltmaking books from RCW Publishing...

## Miniature to Masterpiece

Perfect Piecing Secrets from a Prizewinning Quiltmaker
by Nancy Johnson-Srebro

*Miniature To Masterpiece* is Nancy Johnson-Srebro's guidebook to the unique world of miniature quiltmaking. Nancy is at the forefront of this exciting art, developing over 40 miniature quilt patterns, many of which are copyrighted. Here is an excerpt from the table of contents-

*Patterns with detailed instructions*: Six Patch Charmer, Ohio Star, Pinwheels in Motion, Pioneer Churn Dash, Birds and Trees, Summer Sailing, Country School House, Lone Star Jewel, Scrappy Geese, Kaleidoscope, Wyoming©, and Never Again.

Nancy's award winning "Never Again!" is featured on the cover. *Miniature to Masterpiece* also contains many color photos within it's 80 pages.

$14.95

## Patches of Time

by Linda Halpin

*Patches of Time* offers a historical perspective of the rich legacy of quiltmaking in America. Learn from Linda how quilting reflects the folklore and traditions of the culture, as she presents quilting, appliqué, and patchwork patterns with variations in their historical contexts - patterns that you can use to create your own quiltmaking legacy.

### Patterns! Patterns! Patterns!

· Quilt-As-You-Go-Log Cabin - crib, single, full, queen

· School House Revisited - cover quilt (templates included)- set with quarter square triangles, set with sashing and alternate plain squares - crib, single, full, queen

· The Bear's Paw (templates included) - crib, single, full, queen

· Whig Rose (hand appliqué)- crib, single, queen, king

· Star and Tulip (with special Hand Appliqué How-To's section) - single, full, full/queen

· Young Man's Fancy - crib, single

*Patches of Time* also includes a chapter on quilting patterns and Linda's invaluable techniques are found in a chapter appropriately named Finishing Finesse. *Patches of Time* is indexed, contains well-researched references and interesting footnotes. Color photos are throughout this 112 page book.

$19.95

## Appliqué a la Mode

by Linda Halpin

*Appliqué a la Mode* takes its name from the popular class series that Linda has taught to lovers of appliqué. This 32-page treasure includes miniatures and blocks reminiscent of Baltimore Album Quilts. You'll find Linda's book to be truly scrumptious - a treat in which quilt lovers just have to indulge themselves!

*Appliqué a la Mode* is sure to interest you with these features:

· Teaches appliqué, ruching, fabric sculpting, broderie perse, super fine stems, sawtooth edging, and other three-dimensional techniques to create heirloom masterpieces.

· Illustrates construction steps and completed blocks with over 70 diagrams and graphics and many color photographs.

· Demonstrates the beauty and romance of three-dimensional blossoms, floral baskets, stems and edgings that grace the most spectacular quilts.

If you think you're in love with the classic beauty of quilting, you'll want to buy *Appliqué a la Mode* to stir your heart and to satisfy your desire to create and admire your own legacy in fabric. Plan your book purchases to include this wonderful treasure of quilting gems.

$9.95

---

*You may purchase these books at fine quilt shops and book stores around the world or call/write to Rebecca.*

REBECCA C. WILBER PUBLISHING COMPANY
RR #3 BOX 44 · OLD POST LANE
COLUMBIA CROSS ROADS, PENNSYLVANIA
16914 · PH (717) 549-3331